SHAPE YOUR FINANCIAL FUTURE

4-Step Guide to True Wealth

A blueprint for financial transformation, providing you with tools to shift your mindset, change your habits, and chart a path towards a financially secure future.

hoardingwealth.com

SHAPE YOUR FINANCIAL FUTURE

4-Step Guide to True Wealth

HoardingWealth

First Printing, 2023

Book Design:
        Interior & Cover by Metagraphic Unlimited.
        https://metagraphicunlimited.com

ISBN: 9798856914305 (paperback)
ISBN: 9798860024250 (paperback) (Spanish Version)

SHAPE YOUR FINANCIAL FUTURE

4-Step Guide to True Wealth

Access a wealth of free resources, tools, and support by joining our online community.

https://hoardingwealth.com/join-the-community/

Shape Your Financial Future is designed for anyone yearning for a life rich in experiences and achievements, no matter how ordinary their daily existence may seem. This is a guide for those who harbor ambitions beyond the routine, who aim to transform dreams into tangible realities, and who wish to craft a lasting legacy for future generations. Embracing the principles laid out in these pages, even the most unassuming can lay the foundation for extraordinary financial growth and personal fulfillment.

"That is what learning is. You suddenly understand something you've understood all your life, but in a new way." — **Doris Lessing**

Contents

Prologue

If you've picked up this book, it's likely you have several burning questions on your mind. "How do I save money?" "Where should I invest my money?" "What's the best strategy to pay off my debt?" and "How do I make an effective budget?" "Can I really change my financial future? Can I grow wealth and make my money work for me?". These are just a few of the queries that have likely been spinning in your mind, and you're far from alone. At HoardingWealth.com, these are among the most frequent inquiries we encounter.

This is not merely a guide to wealth accumulation; it's a blueprint for financial transformation, providing you with the tools to shift your mindset, change your habits, and chart a path towards a financially secure future.

In these pages, you will find the wisdom garnered from experiences, distilled into practical steps that will empower you to accumulate wealth in a way that aligns with your unique financial portrait. We'll take the journey step by step, starting by awakening your financial consciousness in 'Financial Awakening.' Then, we'll redefine your perception of wealth, and gradually build your financial skills, from budgeting to investing. The aim is to provide you with the toolset you need to navigate the financial landscape of your life, no matter how rough or smooth it might be.

This book is a map leading to a wealthier and fulfilling life—not just financially, but holistically. It's about defining what success means to you and understanding how wealth accumulation can be a catalyst to reach that definition.

This journey you're about to embark on is not a mere sprint—it's a marathon. It requires persistence, resilience, and determination. But as you persist, not only are you amassing wealth, but you're also establishing a foundation for a legacy that can endure for generations to come.

By the end of this journey, you'll have the knowledge to take control of your financial life. You'll be armed with practical skills to budget, invest, and plan your finances. And it's not just about theory - this book is a practical guide full of action-oriented advice. You'll learn to translate your financial dreams into achievable goals and, in turn, those goals into action.

But you'll gain more than just financial prowess. As your mindset shifts, you'll see money in a new light, not just as a means to an end, but as a tool for growth, opportunity, and freedom. And let me tell you, there's nothing more empowering than that.

As you apply the principles in this book, you'll witness your financial health improving. Debts will decrease, savings will grow, and investments will flourish. And the best part? As your financial narrative changes, you'll inspire others to do the same.

How To Read This Book

Welcome to your personal guide to Hoarding Wealth. I'm thrilled you've chosen this book, a testament to your commitment to taking control of your financial future.

This book is not meant to be skimmed through passively; it's designed as an interactive manual that calls upon you to engage, introspect, and act. So, as you turn each page, remember that you are not just reading—you are participating in your own financial transformation.

I recommend starting with a fresh notebook or journal to accompany you on this journey. This will serve as a companion where you can record your insights, takeaways, and personal reflections. As you navigate through each chapter, you'll come across exercises, workshop tasks, and reflection questions designed to stimulate your thinking and consolidate your learning. Treat these moments as opportunities for self-discovery, jotting down your responses in your notebook. It's through these personalized insights that the abstract concepts of financial wisdom take on a tangible form that is uniquely yours.

Engaging with this book is also about commitment—a commitment to yourself and your future. Remember the saying, "If you always do what you've always done, you'll always get what you've always got." The path to wealth accumulation requires changes in habits, mindset, and actions. You'll find the strategies and insights here to guide those changes, but the implementation is in your hands. It's up to you to translate this knowledge into meaningful action.

The sequence that you will find in this book is intentional, designed to progressively build your financial acumen, starting with basic principles and gradually delving into more advanced concepts and actions. However, remember that this journey is yours to tailor. Feel free to move at your own pace, revisiting previous chapters as needed, and spending more time on areas that you find particularly challenging or intriguing.

As you embark on this journey, remember: this is more than just a book. It's a partner in your quest for financial wisdom, a manual for action, and a catalyst for transformation. Immerse yourself fully in this experience, and let's commence this exciting journey towards becoming a successful wealth accumulator.

CHAPTER 1

Financial Awakening

Let's talk about wealth

Wealth, in its simplest form, is the abundance of valuable resources or valuable material possessions. However, in the context of personal finance, wealth is often defined as the total value of one's assets minus liabilities. These assets can include cash, investments, real estate, and other forms of property.

But wealth is more than just the accumulation of money or assets. It's about financial security and freedom. It's about having the means to provide for your needs and wants, the ability to weather financial storms, and the freedom to make choices that enhance your life quality.

Now, let's delve into the concept of 'Hoarding Wealth'. The term 'hoarding' often carries negative connotations, associated with the excessive accumulation of items. However, when we talk about hoarding wealth, we're referring to a strategic and purposeful process of accumulating and preserving wealth over time.

Hoarding Wealth is about more than just saving money. It is about making your money work for you through smart investments that generate more money to continue investing in new assets. It's about growing and protecting your wealth against inflation and economic downturns. It's about building a financial legacy that can provide for you, your family, and even future generations.

Hoarding wealth benefits not only you and your family but also society as a whole. Here's how:

- **Financial Security for Your Family.** Hoarding wealth ensures that your family is financially secure. It provides a safety net for emergencies, funds for your children's education, and resources for your retirement.

- **Generational Wealth.** Hoarded wealth can be passed down to future generations, providing them with a financial head start. This generational wealth can break the cycle of poverty and contribute to long-term family prosperity.

- **Economic Stability.** On a larger scale, individuals who hoard wealth contribute to economic stability. Their investments fuel businesses, support job creation, and can even contribute to community development.

- **Philanthropy.** Those who have hoarded wealth often have the means to give back to society through philanthropy. They can support causes they care about and make a significant impact in their communities.

In essence, hoarding wealth is a journey of financial growth and security. It's a path that leads to personal freedom, family prosperity, and societal advancement. It's not a selfish act, but a strategic process that benefits many. This is the journey we aim to guide you in this book.

Some misconceptions about wealth

One of the most pervasive misconceptions about wealth is equating it with a high income. In the pursuit of financial freedom, many people believe that the key lies in earning more money. They chase after higher salaries, more lucrative business deals, and bigger profits, all in the hope of securing a financially free future. However, what most fail to realize is that the secret to wealth accumulation isn't necessarily in how much money you make, but in how you manage it. Even with a high income, without the right habits and relationship with money, financial freedom remains elusive. In fact, it's not uncommon to find that those with higher incomes simply have bigger debts.

While earning a high income can certainly provide more opportunities for wealth accumulation, it is not a guarantee. A high income can often lead to lifestyle inflation, where increased spending matches (or even exceeds) increased income. This leaves little room for savings and investments, the true drivers of wealth accumulation.

The truth is, wealth accumulation is possible for anyone, regardless of their income level. It's not about how much money you make, but how you manage it. With the right financial habits, mindset, and a commitment to continuous learning, anyone can become wealthy.

Another common misconception is the belief that wealth comes from a windfall, such as inheriting money or winning the lottery. While these events can certainly boost one's financial status, they are neither reliable nor sustainable paths to wealth. In fact, stories abound of lottery winners or inheritors who end up in financial ruin due to poor money management skills. Without the right financial habits and mindset, a sudden influx of money can lead to reckless spending and unwise investments.

There's also a misconception that wealth is about amassing material possessions. Expensive cars, luxury homes, designer clothes - these are often seen as symbols of wealth. However, these material possessions, while nice to have, do not constitute true wealth. They are liabilities that depreciate over time and do not contribute to wealth accumulation. True wealth lies in assets - things that appreciate over time and generate income, such as investments, real estate, or a profitable business.

Alex and Bailey

To illustrate this point, let's delve into the lives of two individuals - Alex and Bailey. Living in the bustling city of New York, they were as different as night and day, yet they shared a common goal - the desire to accumulate wealth and achieve financial freedom. Their stories serve as a testament to the fact that wealth accumulation isn't just about how much money you make, but more importantly, how you manage it.

Alex was a high-flying executive in a multinational corporation. He earned a handsome salary, lived in a swanky apartment in Manhattan, and drove a luxury car. From the outside, Alex seemed to have it all. However, despite his high income, Alex was living paycheck to paycheck. His lifestyle expenses, coupled with a lack of saving and investing habits, left him with little to no wealth accumulation. He was rich, but he wasn't a wealth accumulator.

On the other side of the city lived Bailey, a school teacher with a modest income. Bailey lived in a small apartment, used public transportation, and led a simple lifestyle. Unlike Alex, Bailey had a different approach to money. She saved diligently, invested wisely, and kept her expenses low. Despite her lower income, Bailey was steadily accumulating wealth and was on the path to financial freedom. She wasn't rich, but she was a wealth accumulator.

Alex and Bailey's stories highlight an important truth about wealth accumulation - it's not about how much money you make, but how you manage it. Alex, despite his high income, was not accumulating wealth due to his poor financial habits. Bailey, on the other hand, was successfully accumulating wealth despite her modest income, thanks to her wise financial habits.

These two tales of financial awakening serve as the starting point of our journey into the world of wealth accumulation. They underscore the importance of the right financial attitude and habits, setting the stage for the Financial Snapshot - the first step in the wealth accumulation journey. As we delve deeper into this journey, we'll discover how to transform from being merely rich, like Alex, to becoming a wealth accumulator, like Bailey.

The Importance of Financial Habits

In the realm of personal finance, habits are the invisible architects of our financial destiny. They silently shape our financial health, sculpting our path towards wealth accumulation or financial stagnation.

Your financial habits are not just routines—they are the driving force that can either propel you towards the fulfillment of your dreams or bind you in a perpetual cycle of financial stress. They determine the outcome of your financial race, acting as the 90% of the momentum that drives you towards victory or defeat in achieving financial freedom.

Consider the habit of saving. It's like a quiet stream, trickling consistently into a reservoir. Over time, this stream fills the reservoir, creating a pool of resources that can be used in times of need or channeled into investment opportunities. The act of saving, done consistently, cultivates a sense of financial discipline, teaching us the art of delayed gratification and protecting us from the pitfalls of excessive spending.

Then, there's the habit of investing. If saving is the stream that fills the reservoir, investing is the force that expands it. Investing takes the money we've saved and puts it to work, generating more money. It's the golden goose of wealth accumulation, laying eggs that can hatch into even more golden geese. Over time, investing can lead to exponential growth of wealth, taking us further on our wealth accumulation journey.

But it's not just about what we're bringing in; it's also about what's going out. Here, the habit of mindful spending comes into play. Mindful spending isn't about penny-pinching or denying ourselves enjoyment. It's about making thoughtful decisions about where our money goes. It's about distinguishing between needs and wants, making intentional purchases, and investing in experiences and items that truly add value to our lives. Mindful spending keeps our financial ship steady, preventing us from sinking into the sea of wasteful expenditure.

However, just as there are habits that build wealth, there are habits that can erode it. Excessive spending, for instance, is like a hole in our financial reservoir, draining away the resources we've worked hard to accumulate. It's a habit that can lead us into the quagmire of debt, hindering our progress towards wealth accumulation.

Similarly, high levels of debt, especially high-interest consumer debt, can act like a financial leech, siphoning away our wealth. It's a burden that weighs us down, making it harder to move forward on our wealth accumulation journey.

Lastly, the lack of planning can leave us wandering in the financial wilderness. Without a budget or a financial plan, we're like sailors adrift at sea, with no map or compass to guide us. Planning gives us direction, helping us navigate towards our financial goals.

Being conscious of your habits—whether they serve your financial goals or impede them—is a critical step in mastering your personal finance. It's about recognizing and rectifying detrimental habits while nurturing and reinforcing beneficial ones. But if you continue on autopilot, oblivious to your financial habits, you risk perpetuating your current circumstances.

In the journey of hoarding wealth, our financial habits are our companions, guiding us towards our destination or leading us astray. Cultivating positive financial habits and shedding negative ones is a crucial part of this journey, shaping our path towards wealth accumulation.

So, take a moment to reflect. Are your habits aligning with your financial aspirations, or are they setting you off course? Remember, if you yearn for different results, you must first change your habits. And the first step towards that transformation begins with awareness. Harness this understanding and use it to reshape your financial habits, so they become powerful tools in your journey towards financial freedom.

The Role of Financial Education

Financial education is more than just learning about money. It's about understanding how money works and how to make it work for you. It's about learning to manage your money effectively, to save wisely, to invest strategically, and to plan for the future. It's about gaining the knowledge and skills to take control of your financial destiny.

It's an exploration into the mechanisms of wealth—it teaches us how money operates and how we can harness it for our benefit. It imparts skills to manage, save, invest, and strategize for your financial future.

Without financial education, we are like sailors trying to navigate without a compass. We can easily find ourselves adrift, making poor financial decisions that lead us further away from our destination of wealth accumulation. We risk becoming trapped in a paycheck-to-paycheck existence, accumulating high-interest debt, or failing to save and invest for the future.

A lack of financial education can also leave us vulnerable to financial scams or unwise investments. Without a solid understanding of financial principles, we might be enticed by get-rich-quick schemes or invest in ventures we don't fully understand, risking our hard-earned money.

Contrastingly, financial education empowers us—We learn to navigate the financial seas with confidence, making informed decisions that move us closer to our goal of wealth accumulation. We learn to recognize and avoid financial pitfalls, and to seize opportunities for growth.

With financial education, we can learn to decipher financial jargon that once seemed insurmountable, making us capable of understanding our tax responsibilities, different types of insurances, retirement plans, and the fine print of loan agreements. It empowers us to engage in intelligent conversations with financial advisors, and to ask the right questions. It grants us the ability to discern sound financial advice from mere sales talk, to identify red flags, and to protect ourselves from potential fraud.

It equips us with a forward-thinking mindset. A financially educated individual does not merely focus on the present. Instead, they strategize and plan for their long-term financial health. They understand the value of building a diverse investment portfolio, the importance of an emergency fund, and the critical role of estate planning.

In a world where financial decisions can significantly impact our lives, having a solid foundation of financial education is not just an asset—it is a necessity. It is the very sail that propels our ship towards the horizon of Hoarding Wealth. Prioritizing financial education ensures we're not merely aimlessly adrift in the financial ocean. Instead, we're charting our course with purpose and precision.

Financial education is not just a stepping stone—it's the cornerstone of financial success. Its importance lies in how it enriches our lives, providing us with the tools to make informed decisions, secure our future, and ultimately, hoard wealth.

Difference Between Being Rich and Accumulating Wealth

In our society, the terms 'rich' and 'wealthy' are often used interchangeably. However, when it comes to financial success, there is a significant difference between being rich and accumulating wealth. Understanding this difference is crucial to your journey towards becoming a wealth accumulator.

Being rich is about having a high income. It's about the flashy lifestyle, the luxury cars, the designer clothes, and the million-dollar homes. It's about living in the moment, enjoying the fruits of your labor, and spending money as fast as you earn it. But being rich doesn't necessarily mean you're financially secure. In fact, many rich people live paycheck to paycheck, always one financial emergency away from disaster. They may look successful on the outside, but their financial situation is often precarious, built on a foundation of debt and financial instability.

Accumulating wealth, on the other hand, is about more than just making money. It's about saving, investing, and growing your money over time. It's about building assets that generate income, even when you're not working. It's about financial security and independence. Wealthy individuals may not live as extravagantly as the rich, but they have something far more valuable: financial freedom. They have the freedom to make choices, to take risks, and to pursue their passions without worrying about money.

The difference between being rich and accumulating wealth can be likened to the difference between sprinting and running a marathon. Being rich is like a sprint. It's fast, exciting, and exhilarating, but it's also short-lived. You can't sprint forever. Eventually, you'll run out of steam and have to stop.

Accumulating wealth is like running a marathon. It's slower and requires more patience and endurance. But it's also more sustainable. You can keep going for much longer, and the rewards at the end of the race are well worth the effort.

So, how do you shift from being rich to accumulating wealth? It starts with changing your mindset. Instead of focusing on earning more, focus on saving and investing more. Instead of spending money on things that depreciate in value, spend money on things that appreciate in value. Instead of living for the moment, plan for the future.

Reflect on Your Financial Goals: Take some time to write down your financial goals. Are they oriented towards appearing rich (buying a luxury car, a big house, designer clothes) or towards accumulating wealth (investing in stocks, buying rental properties, starting a business)? This exercise can help you understand your current mindset and identify areas where you might need to shift your focus.

Analyze Your Spending Habits: Look at your bank statements or use a budgeting app to analyze where your money is going. Are you spending on items that depreciate in value (like a new car or the latest smartphone) or are you investing in assets that could potentially increase your wealth over time (like stocks, bonds, or real estate)? This analysis can give you a clear picture of whether your spending habits are aligned with wealth accumulation.

Visualize Your Ideal Lifestyle: Imagine your life 5, 10, or 20 years from now. What does it look like? Are you living a lavish lifestyle, constantly chasing after the latest trends, or are you living comfortably, with a strong financial foundation and the freedom to do what you love without worrying about money? This visualization exercise can help you understand what truly matters to you and guide your financial decisions.

Societal misconceptions often glorify the rich lifestyle while overlooking the benefits of wealth accumulation. We're bombarded with images of celebrities and influencers living lavish lifestyles, leading many to equate success with high spending. However, this narrative fails to highlight the financial insecurity that often accompanies such a lifestyle.

In contrast, wealth accumulation is less visible and less glamorous, but it offers a path to lasting financial security and freedom. By understanding this, you can resist societal pressures to spend and instead focus on building your wealth.

In the end, the choice between being rich and accumulating wealth is a personal one. But by understanding the difference, you can make informed decisions that align with your long-term financial goals.

The Journey Ahead

As we turn the page on this first chapter, we stand at the threshold of an exciting journey - a journey that will transform not just your finances, but your entire attitude towards wealth. This journey is not a sprint, but a marathon, requiring patience, persistence, and a willingness to learn and grow.

Our journey will unfold in three distinct stages - The Financial Snapshot, The Wealth Wisdom Workshop and The Prosperity Pursuit. Each stage is designed to guide you deeper into the realm of wealth accumulation.

Reflection Questions/Exercises

As we close this chapter, I invite you to reflect on your own financial journey. Remember that notebook or journal I mentioned earlier? Now's the perfect time to put it to good use. It will serve as a valuable tool for introspection and self-evaluation, an essential companion on your path to hoarding wealth.

I encourage you to delve deep and answer the following questions with utmost honesty and sincerity. Remember, any deception in this exercise is a deception to yourself, derailing your journey even before it begins. It's crucial that you confront these questions truthfully—your future financial health depends on it.

1. How would you define wealth in your own terms?
2. How do you perceive the concept of 'hoarding wealth'? Do you see it as a positive or negative practice?
3. What is your current strategy for wealth accumulation? How effective do you think it is?
4. Do you identify more with Alex or Bailey? Why?
5. What steps are you currently taking to manage your money wisely, like Bailey, instead of just earning more, like Alex?
6. What financial habits do you think you need to improve to start accumulating wealth?
7. How can your wealth, if appropriately managed and accumulated, benefit your family and society as a whole?
8. How do you feel about the concept of generational wealth? Is it something you aspire to?
9. Do you have a financial safety net in place? If not, what steps can you take to create one?
10. How are you investing your income to generate more wealth and secure your future?
11. What kind of financial legacy do you want to leave for future generations?
12. What are the obstacles or challenges that you think may hinder your

journey to wealth accumulation?

13. Do you find it difficult to change a financial habit? If so, why? and what might help you in overcoming this challenge?

14. On a scale of 1 to 10, how would you rate your current level of financial education?

15. In what areas of finance do you feel confident, and in what areas do you feel you need to improve your knowledge?

16. What steps can you take to improve your financial education?

17. Consider your current financial habits. Are they serving you well on your path to wealth accumulation, or are they hindering your progress?

18. Imagine your life 10 years from now. Are your current financial habits and decisions leading you towards that vision? If not, what changes might you need to make?

19. What changes might you need to make to align your habits with your financial goals?

20. Reflect on your current lifestyle. Would you categorize it more closely aligned with being rich or accumulating wealth? Why?

21. What are some spending habits you've noticed in your life that are more associated with being 'rich' than being 'wealthy'?

22. How has your perspective on wealth and richness changed after reading this chapter?

If you've been focusing more on appearing rich, what steps can you take to shift your mindset towards wealth accumulation?
If you have been more focused on the 'rich' lifestyle, what fears or concerns do you have about shifting towards wealth accumulation?

Remember, this journey is not about perfection, but progress. It's about making small, consistent changes that add up to big results. So, as we embark on this journey together, I encourage you to approach it with an open mind, a willing heart, and a commitment to your financial growth and freedom.

CHAPTER 2

The Financial Snapshot

The journey to wealth accumulation begins with one crucial step, understanding your current financial situation. This is where the concept of a Financial Snapshot comes into play. A financial snapshot is a complete description of your current financial situation, including your income, expenses, debt, and savings. It's like taking a picture of your finances at a particular moment in time.

A financial snapshot is just as important as it provides a clear and objective picture of your financial position. It's easy to get a vague idea of your income and expenses, or a rough estimate of your savings. But without hard numbers, it's impossible to make informed financial decisions or set realistic financial goals.

Creating a financial snapshot may seem like a daunting task, especially for those people who don't like math, or maybe if you've never done it before, but if you're reading this book, it's because you really want a change in your life, a change that you have a future with less financial stress, and with that desire, I am sure that it will be very easy for you to do this simple task. It is an essential first step on the path to wealth accumulation. It provides a solid foundation on which you can build your financial future.

Once you have your Financial Snapshot, you can use it to make better financial decisions. You can identify areas where you can cut back, opportunities to increase your income, and strategies to pay off debt faster. You can also use it to set realistic financial goals, like saving for a down payment on a house, paying off your student loans, or taking early retirement.

Your Financial Snapshot

Now that we understand the importance of a Financial Snapshot, let's dive into the process of creating one. Don't worry, we'll break it down into manageable steps.

- **Gather Your Financial Information**: Start by gathering all your financial information. This includes bank statements, credit card statements, loan documents, pay stubs, and any other documents that provide information about your income, expenses, debts, and savings.

- **List Your Income**: Next, list all your sources of income. This includes not just your salary or business revenue, but also any side hustles, rental income, dividends, alimony, child support, social security benefits, among others. Ensure to consider after-tax amounts to get a real sense of your disposable income.

- **List Your Expenses**: Now, list all your expenses. Start with your fixed expenses, such as rent or mortgage payments, utility bills, car payments, and insurance premiums. Then, list your variable expenses, such as groceries, gas, dining out, entertainment, and personal care. Don't forget to include occasional expenses, such as car maintenance or medical bills. Add up all these expenses to find your total monthly expenses.

- **List Your Debts**: If you have any debts, list them next. Include the total amount owed, the interest rate, and the minimum monthly payment for each debt.

- **List Your Savings**: Finally, list all your savings. This includes savings accounts, retirement accounts, investment accounts, cash and any other savings you have.

Now, subtract your total expenses and total debts from your total income.

The result is your net income. If your net income is positive, you're living within your means. If it's negative, you're living beyond your means and need to make some real changes.

Common mistakes to avoid

As we wrap up this insightful chapter on building your financial snapshot, it's important that we highlight and address some of the common mistakes often found in this process. By recognizing these potential mistakes, you'll be well prepared to navigate them.

Underestimation of small expenses: It's all too easy to trivialize the impact of those seemingly insignificant daily expenses. That morning coffee, the lottery ticket, the occasional takeout, the tips you leave, those unplanned purchases, each of these may not seem like much on their own. But when collected over the course of a month, they often add a surprising amount to your expenses. When sketching out your financial picture, don't discount these smaller expenses. Every penny counts and plays a role in putting together an accurate financial picture.

Missing irregular but significant expenses is an all-too-often overlooked financial planning mistake. These could include annual insurance premiums, vehicle maintenance, or unexpected home repair costs. While these don't show up on your monthly bills, their impact on your yearly financial health can be substantial. To account for them, calculate these expenses annually and then divide them into a monthly allowance.

Leisure and personal entertainment do not escape monthly expenses and should not be ignored in financial planning. From your Netflix subscription to your weekend getaways, your hobbies, and even your favorite treats at the coffee shop, they all deserve a place in your Financial Snapshot. They are as much a part of your financial life as utility bills or mortgage payments.

Many make the mistake of assuming that their finances remain constant throughout the year. However, a host of factors, such as seasonal variations, vacations, annual bonuses, or tax returns, can cause fluctuations in your income and expenses. Avoid this oversimplification and embrace the dynamism of your financial cycle throughout the year.

Avoiding these common mistakes will ensure that you build a more accurate and practical financial snapshot. Your goal here is to gain an unequivocal and complete understanding of your financial health, forming a solid foundation for all future financial strategies and decisions. And remember, it's not about perfection, it's about progress and proactive planning. So, as you go forward, keep these potential pitfalls in mind, and you'll be well on your way to creating an effective financial roadmap.

Reflection Questions/Exercises

At the end of the exercise your current financial snapshot should look like the figure below.

Assets	Amount	Liabilities	Amount
Cash & Cash Equivalent		Short Term Credit	
Total Cash & Cash Equivalent	$	Total Short term Credit	$
Brokerage & Retirement Accounts		Loan & Mortgages	
Total Brokerage & Retirement Accounts	$		
Properties			
		Total Loan & Mortgages	$
		Other Liabilities	
		Total Other Liabilities	$
Total Properties	$	Total Liabilities	$
Other Assets			

Grand Total

Grand Total = Total Assets - Total Liabilities

Total Assets	$
Total Liabilities	$
Grand Total	$

Total Other Assets	$

The previous table summarizes all the information about your income, expenses, debts, and savings. Comparing these values will help you understand your financial health and make informed decisions about your financial future.

Finally, as a step beyond the snapshot, it's essential to understand that this financial snapshot is not static. It changes over time as your income, expenses, savings, and debts fluctuate. Therefore, it's crucial to revisit and update your financial snapshot regularly, at least once or twice a year, to keep track of your progress and adjust your financial plan as needed.

Analyzing your Financial snapshot

Now that you've taken a thorough look at your Financial Snapshot, take a moment to breathe. Understanding our financial health can be daunting and it's okay if the picture isn't perfect. Let's reflect on what you've uncovered.

Are the numbers looking back at you familiar, or are they a surprise? Maybe you're feeling a sense of relief, validation, or perhaps, discomfort. Whatever your reaction, recognize it's a crucial step forward in understanding your financial well-being.

Regardless of the emotions that this exercise might have stirred up, remember that knowledge is power. You're now better equipped to steer your financial ship than you were before this exercise. This Snapshot is not just a collection of numbers—it's a mirror, reflecting the reality of your current financial situation, unclouded by guesswork or assumptions.

Now, why is this important? Your Financial Snapshot is the compass that will guide your financial decisions moving forward—it is your starting point. It serves as the grounding truth in your financial journey, guiding you towards your goals while keeping your feet firmly planted in reality.

If you find yourself in a positive net income position, congratulations! This indicates you're living within your means. Your challenge now is to maintain this status, and possibly, look into avenues for further growth, investments, and savings.

On the other hand, if your net income is negative or almost negative, take heart. This exercise has illuminated areas of your finances that need attention, which is a vital step towards improvement. The path towards a positive net income might involve a combination of cutting back on expenses, paying off debts, or increasing your income streams.

Regardless of your situation, your Financial Snapshot will help you reassess your goals and aspirations. Maybe you're saving for a new home, planning for a comfortable retirement, or looking to start a business. Each of these goals requires financial planning and execution. Your Snapshot not only provides a clear picture of where you stand today but also helps in paving the way towards where you want to be.

Remember, your Financial Snapshot is not static; it's a dynamic, ever-changing entity. As your life circumstances change, so will your Snapshot. Revisit and update it periodically to reflect your current reality and use it as a vital tool to navigate the financial landscape of your life.

Understanding our finances is not always comfortable, but it's essential. Now that you have your Financial Snapshot, you're no longer flying blind. You've switched on the headlights, illuminating the path towards financial stability, growth, and ultimately, prosperity.

In this book, we'll delve into strategies for adjusting and improving your Financial Snapshot, setting you on the right track towards achieving your financial goals. But for now, give yourself a pat on the back—you've taken a big step towards financial clarity and empowerment.

Reflection Questions/Exercises

It is time to reflect on what you have just absorbed. If you've diligently followed the steps outlined in this book, it signifies that you are truly committed to transforming your financial future - and for that, congratulations! Now, let's take that notebook or journal of yours once again and delve into some deep introspection.

These questions are designed to invoke thought, to clarify your financial understanding, and to enable you to take purposeful steps towards achieving your goals. This type of exercise is intended to help you convert the knowledge you've acquired into actionable insights. It encourages you to reflect on your current financial circumstances, identify areas that require improvement, and devise practical strategies to attain financial success. Now, let's dive into these questions:

1. Do you feel satisfied or dissatisfied with the result of your net income and why?
2. What are all the different sources of income you currently have? Are there any potential sources of income that you could explore?
3. Which expenses could you potentially reduce?
4. Consider your savings. How much are you currently saving each month? How much would you like to save?
5. What does this snapshot tell you about your current financial situation?
6. Reflecting on your financial snapshot, what are some financial goals you could set for yourself?

Identify one area from your financial snapshot you would like to improve over the next three months. What specific actions will you take to make this improvement?

Do you think your net income will be enough to save, invest and entertain your loved ones every month?
As you examine your financial snapshot, take a moment to acknowledge

your feelings towards it. Do you feel like a slave to your job, ensnared by debt, or a captive to your indulgences? Alternatively, do you feel liberated by your financial decisions, content with your progress, or perhaps feel like you're excessively tethered to savings? Articulate why you identify with these emotions and how you aspire to feel in your financial future. Remember, there's no right or wrong answer here – it's about understanding your current state and envisioning your desired emotional and financial landscape.

CHAPTER 3

Wealth Wisdom Workshop

Welcome to the Wealth Wisdom Workshop, the second stage of our journey towards wealth accumulation. This is where we delve into the heart of financial knowledge, equipping ourselves with the wisdom and tools needed to navigate the path to hoarding wealth.

This workshop is the culmination of countless hours of research, analysis, and real-world experience. It's the product of years spent exploring the intricacies of personal finance, studying the habits of successful wealth accumulators, and learning from the triumphs and failures of those who've embarked on this journey before us.

But more than that, it's a reflection of the countless stories and experiences shared by you, our readers. Your questions, your struggles, your successes, and your insights have been invaluable in shaping this workshop. Each topic, each concept, and each strategy has been influenced by your journey towards wealth accumulation.

As I sit here, pouring over the data and feedback we've collected over the years, I'm struck by the recurring themes that emerge. The most frequently asked questions that our users have are: "How do I save money?", "Ho w do I invest my money?", "How do I pay off my debt?", and "How do I budget my money?" These questions, so simple yet so profound, are the building blocks of financial freedom.

And yet, despite the abundance of information available in this digital age, these fundamental questions remain largely unanswered for many. The main goals of people continue to be buying a house, getting out of debt, and saving for retirement. In the middle of the 21st century, as a society, we still grapple with the same financial challenges as we did a hundred years ago. This, to me, is both surprising and deeply concerning.

It's a bit like being in a room full of cookbooks but still not knowing how to boil an egg. We're in the age of information, yet we're still scratching our heads over the same financial questions our great-grandparents probably had. It's as if we've been given the keys to the library, but we're still stuck on the first page of the 'Financial Literacy 101' textbook.

It's clear that financial education is not just a luxury, but a necessity. It's not something to be sought after when the noose of debt is already around our necks, but a tool to be wielded proactively, to prevent financial hardship and secure a prosperous future.

That's why we've created this workshop. It's not just a response to these questions, but a comprehensive guide to financial freedom. It's a roadmap to wealth accumulation, answering these fundamental questions and teaching you how to set goals that multiply your wealth.

As we embark on this journey of learning, remember that this is not a dry, academic exercise. This is a journey of discovery, of awakening, of transformation. It's about making financial knowledge not just something we know, but something we live with.

We'll explore the mindset of a wealth accumulator, how to set goals that generate wealth, how to budget, the role of saving and investing in wealth accumulation, and the power of financial attitude. We'll delve into the intricacies of our money personalities and learn how to shift our mindset to become successful wealth accumulators. We'll discuss the importance of financial resilience and the role it plays in our journey towards wealth accumulation.

But this workshop is more than just a collection of financial concepts and strategies. It's a call to action. It's a challenge to take control of your financial future, to make the conscious decision to become a wealth accumulator. It's an invitation to embark on a journey of financial transformation, to shift your mindset, change your habits, and embrace the principles of wealth accumulation.

So, as we delve into the heart of financial knowledge, I invite you to approach this workshop with an open mind and a willingness to learn. I encourage you to engage with the material, to ask questions, to challenge assumptions, and to apply what you learn to your own financial journey.

Remember, the path to wealth accumulation is not a straight line. It's filled with twists and turns, ups and downs. But with the right knowledge, the right mindset, and the right strategies, you can navigate this path successfully and reach your destination of financial freedom.

Understanding Your Money Personality

Our relationship with money is a complex one, shaped by a myriad of factors ranging from our upbringing to our personal experiences. It's a relationship that begins in childhood, as we observe how the adults around us handle money and continues to evolve as we navigate our own financial journey. This relationship, and the attitudes and behaviors it engenders, forms what we call our 'money personality'.

Your money personality is a reflection of how you view and interact with money. It influences how you save, spend, invest, and even how you feel about money. Understanding your money personality is the first step towards reshaping your financial habits and embarking on your journey towards wealth accumulation.

But how do you identify your money personality? And once you've identified it, how do you shift your mindset to become a successful wealth accumulator? These are the questions we'll be exploring in this section.

To identify your money personality, you need to reflect on your attitudes and behaviors towards money. Consider the following questions:

How do you feel about money? Is it a source of stress or comfort for you? How do you handle money? Are you a saver or a spender? How do you approach financial decisions? Do you plan and research, or do you make decisions on the spur of the moment? How do you view wealth? Is it a goal, a measure of success, or something else entirely? Your answers to these questions will give you insights into your money personality. They'll help you understand your strengths and weaknesses when it comes to managing money, and they'll highlight the areas you need to work on to become a successful wealth hoarder.

Let's start some self-reflection. I want you to try to answer these questions honestly, and I will help you with some exercises for each question.

How do you feel about money? Is it a source of stress or comfort for you? This question is about your emotional relationship with money. Some people see money as a source of security and comfort. They feel at ease when they have money in the bank and stress when they don't. Others see money as a source of stress, regardless of how much they have. They worry about losing it, spending it, or not having enough of it.

For example, if the thought of checking your bank account gives you heart palpitations, you might have a stress-based relationship with money. On the other hand, if you feel a sense of calm and security when you think about money, you likely have a comfort-based relationship with it.

Exercise: Take a moment to reflect on your feelings about money. Write down any emotions that come up when you think about money. Are they positive or negative? Do you feel calm or anxious? This exercise will help you understand your emotional relationship with money.

How do you handle money? Are you a saver or a spender?

This question is about your financial behaviors. Some people are natural savers. They enjoy watching their savings grow and feel uncomfortable spending money. Others are natural spenders. They enjoy the thrill of buying new things and find it hard to resist a good deal.

For example, if you find yourself frequently checking your savings account and feeling a sense of satisfaction when you see the balance increase, you're likely a saver. If, on the other hand, you find yourself frequently browsing online stores and feeling a sense of excitement when you make a purchase, you're likely to spend.

Exercise: Reflect on your spending and saving habits. Do you find it easier to save money or to spend it? Do you get more satisfaction from seeing your savings grow or from buying new things? Write down your thoughts. Write it down, this will help you understand whether you're a saver or a spender.

How do you approach financial decisions? Do you plan and research, or do you make decisions on the spur of the moment?

This question is about your decision-making process. Some people are careful planners. They research, compare options, and think carefully before making a financial decision. Others are impulsive. They make decisions on the spur of the moment, often based on their emotions or immediate desires.

For example, if you're the type of person who spends hours researching before making a purchase, you're likely a planner. If you often find yourself making impulsive purchases based on your emotions or immediate desires, you're likely an impulsive decision-maker.

Exercise: Reflect on your decision-making process. Do you tend to plan and research before making a financial decision, or do you often make decisions on the spur of the moment? Write down your thoughts. This will help you understand your decision-making style.

How do you view wealth? Is it a goal, a measure of success, or something else entirely?

This question is about your perception of wealth. Some people view wealth as a goal to be achieved. They strive to accumulate wealth and measure their success by their financial assets. Others view wealth as a tool for achieving other goals, such as providing for their family, traveling the world, or making a difference in their community.

For example, if you dream of having a certain amount of money in the bank, owning a luxury car, or living in a big house, you likely see wealth as a goal. If, on the other hand, you dream of using money to provide a good education for your children, travel to new places, or support causes you care about, you would likely see wealth as a tool.

Exercise: Reflect on your perception of wealth. Do you see it as a goal to be achieved, a measure of success, or a tool for achieving other goals? Write down your thoughts. This will help you understand your view of wealth.

Your answers to these questions will give you insights into your money personality. They'll help you understand your strengths and weaknesses when it comes to managing money, and they'll highlight the areas you need to work on to become a successful wealth accumulator.

Now, I know this self-reflection can be a bit daunting. It's like looking into a financial mirror, and sometimes, we might not like what we see. But remember, this is not about judging or criticizing ourselves. It's about understanding ourselves better so we can make positive changes.

Understanding your financial personality is a crucial step on your journey to wealth accumulation. It's about knowing where you are now so you can plan where you want to go. So, take your time with these exercises. Write your answers in your notebook, this is what the workshop is about, reflect on it and when you're ready, keep reading.

From the questions and exercises listed above, we can infer several broad categories of "money personalities." But remember, these are not mutually exclusive, and you may exhibit traits from more than one category. They can also change over time due to life experiences or conscious efforts to alter financial behaviors.

- **The Saver**: Savers get a sense of satisfaction and security from watching their bank balance grow. They are generally cautious with their money and are less likely to make impulsive purchases. Saving for the future is a priority, and they tend to live within or below their means.

- **The Spender**: Spenders enjoy the thrill of buying and find satisfaction in owning new things. They are more likely to make impulsive purchases and might struggle with saving money. For spenders, money is there to be enjoyed in the present, even if that sometimes comes at the cost of future financial security.

- **The Worrier**: For the Worrier, money is often a source of stress. They might have plenty of money in the bank but still worry about financial security. This anxiety might lead them to be overly cautious with their money, sometimes to the point of not enjoying the benefits their money could bring.

- **The Strategist**: Strategists tend to approach financial decisions carefully. They research, plan, and think about the potential outcomes before making a decision. Money is a tool to achieve their long-term goals, and they are likely to have a financial plan in place.

- **The Optimist**: Optimists tend to be relaxed about money. They might not have much in savings, but they believe they can earn more when they need to. They might be prone to impulsive spending, relying on their ability to earn more money in the future to cover their expenses.

- **The Goal-Oriented**: For these individuals, wealth is a measure of success and a goal to be achieved. They are motivated by financial milestones, such as reaching a certain net worth or buying a dream home. They are likely to have clear financial goals and work hard to achieve them.

- **The Philanthropist**: Those with the Philanthropist money personality see wealth as a tool to help others and make a difference in the world. They are likely to contribute to causes they care about and might prioritize giving even when their own financial situation isn't robust.

Understanding your money personality is a big step in changing your financial habits. Once you recognize your strengths and weaknesses, you can take steps to improve your financial behaviors and work toward your financial goals.

For instance, if you identify as having a 'Worrier' money personality, you might find that you're constantly worried about not having enough money, even if you're earning a decent income. This could lead to behaviors such as excessive saving or frugality, which might prevent you from enjoying your money in the present.

However, being aware of this trait can help you devise a financial plan that addresses this stress. You might find it helpful to set up an emergency fund, for example. Knowing you have a safety net can alleviate financial stress and allow you to make more balanced financial decisions.

On the other hand, if you have a conservative like 'Saver' money personality, you might be risk-averse and hesitant to invest your money, preferring to keep it in a savings account instead. While this can be a safe approach, it might also prevent your wealth from growing as much as it could.

In this case, understanding your conservative tendencies can help you create a financial plan that gently pushes your comfort zone. You might start by investing a small amount of money in low-risk investments, gradually increasing your comfort level with investing.

Ah, but if you came out with the 'spender' money personality. This is a personality type that enjoys the thrill of making purchases, often prioritizing immediate gratification over long-term financial goals. If you identify with this personality type, you might find yourself frequently in debt or living paycheck to paycheck, despite having a substantial income.

However, being a spender isn't necessarily a bad thing. It means you value experiences and the joy that comes from buying things you love. The key is to balance this tendency with sound financial habits.

If you're a spender, your financial plan might involve setting strict budgets for discretionary spending. You could allocate a certain amount of your income to 'fun money' – money you're free to spend on whatever you want, guilt-free. The rest of your income could then be allocated towards necessities, savings, and investments.

You might also find it helpful to set up automatic transfers to your savings or investment accounts. This way, a portion of your income is automatically set aside before you have a chance to spend it.

Another strategy is to find ways to satisfy your love for spending without breaking the bank. This could involve hunting for bargains, buying second-hand items, or swapping clothes or goods with friends.

Remember, the goal isn't to change your money personality, but to understand it and work with it. By doing so, you can create a financial plan that aligns with your personality and supports your journey towards wealth accumulation.

Wealth Accumulator's Mindset

The mindset of a wealth accumulator is a fascinating study of psychology, discipline, and strategy. It's a mindset that sets the stage for financial success and prosperity.

Wealth accumulators view money differently. They see it not as an end, but as a means to an end. Money, to them, is a tool that can be wielded to create more wealth. It's a seed that, when planted and nurtured, can grow into a towering tree of abundance. This perspective is a stark contrast to the common view of money as a finite resource to be spent and enjoyed in the present.

The wealth accumulator's mindset is also characterized by a long-term vision. They are not swayed by the ebb and flow of the market or the allure of quick profits. Instead, they remain steadfast in their journey, understanding that wealth accumulation is a marathon, not a sprint. They are the tortoise in the race, slow and steady, but ultimately victorious.

Discipline and patience are the hallmarks of a wealth accumulator. They resist the temptation of instant gratification, choosing instead to delay pleasure for long-term gain. They understand the power of compound interest and the value of consistent saving and investing. They are not deterred by temporary setbacks, knowing that the path to wealth is often paved with challenges.

Continuous learning is another key trait of wealth accumulators. They are always seeking to expand their knowledge and understanding of financial matters. They read books, attend seminars, listen to podcasts, and engage in conversations about money and investing. They understand that knowledge is power, and in the world of finance, it's the power to make informed decisions that lead to wealth accumulation.

Consider the story of Warren Buffett, one of the most successful investors of all time. Buffett bought his first stock at the age of 11 and has since amassed a fortune of over $100 billion. But what sets Buffett apart is not just his wealth, but his mindset. He is known for his long-term investment strategy, his discipline, and his insatiable thirst for knowledge. He once said, "I just sit in my office and read all day." This continuous learning, combined with patience and discipline, has been key to his success.

But let's also look at some facts. A study by Thomas J. Stanley and William D. Danko, authors of "The Millionaire Next Door," found that most millionaires are ordinary people with ordinary jobs. They accumulate wealth not by earning high incomes, but by living frugally, saving diligently, and investing wisely. This underscores the importance of the wealth accumulator's mindset.

They don't fear it or view it as a necessary evil. Instead, they respect it, understand its value, and use it to create opportunities and security for themselves and their loved ones.

Shift to Your New Mindset

The power of the mind is an incredible thing. Our thoughts and beliefs shape our actions, and our actions, in turn, shape our reality. This is especially true when it comes to wealth accumulation.

Take the example of Elon Musk. He once said, "When something is important enough, you do it even if the odds are not in your favor." His belief in the importance of sustainable energy and space exploration led him to found Tesla and SpaceX, despite numerous challenges and setbacks.

These illustrate the power of the mind in shaping our reality. But you don't have to be a billionaire to harness this power. Even small shifts in mindset can have a big impact on your financial journey.

If you believe that you're bad with money, you're likely to make poor financial decisions that reinforce this belief. But if you start to believe that you can be good with money, you'll start to make better financial decisions. You'll start saving more, spending less, and investing wisely. Over time, these actions will lead to wealth accumulation.

The same applies to your beliefs about wealth. If you believe that wealth is something that's out of reach for you, you're unlikely to take the steps necessary to accumulate wealth. But if you believe that you can become wealthy, you'll be motivated to take these steps.

So, how can you harness the power of your mind to accumulate wealth? This isn't a fleeting change or an overnight metamorphosis, but a gradual process of challenging and reshaping your existing beliefs about money. It's about replacing detrimental behaviors with beneficial ones and adopting the habits and attitudes of successful wealth accumulators.

To better illustrate which mindset we should adopt, it is also important to know which one is not, to have a good mindset, we are going to examine these two visions in a general way.

A 'wrong' mindset, in terms of wealth accumulation, is one that holds you back from achieving your financial goals. It's characterized by negative beliefs and behaviors such as overspending, not saving, avoiding financial planning, and harboring a scarcity mindset - the belief that there's never enough money. This mindset often leads to financial stress and prevents wealth accumulation.

On the other hand, a 'good' or 'wealthy' mindset is one that promotes financial well-being and wealth accumulation. It's characterized by positive beliefs and behaviors such as mindful spending, regular saving, strategic investing, and an abundance mindset - the belief that there's always enough money and opportunities to make more. This mindset leads to financial freedom and wealth accumulation.

Depending on your money personality, you might need to adopt different strategies to shift your mindset. Changing your mindset based on your money personality involves understanding your current attitudes towards money and then consciously shifting them towards healthier, more productive beliefs. Here's how you can do it for each money personality:

The Spender: If you're a spender, you might believe that money is for enjoyment and there's always more where that came from. To shift your mindset, start viewing money as a tool for building wealth rather than just a means for immediate gratification. Practice delaying gratification and focusing on long-term financial goals, this is the real key for you, long-term goals that really mean something that you care enough to keep you motivated throughout the process.

The Saver: If you're a saver, you might believe that money provides security and the more you have saved, the better. While saving is a good habit, being overly cautious can prevent you from taking calculated risks that could grow your wealth, like investing. Shift your mindset to understand that strategic risk-taking is a part of wealth accumulation. The key to the mental change that this type of personality needs is knowledge. Learning more about investments will give you the tools and security you need to make your money grow.

The Worrier: If you're a 'worrier' debtor, you might believe that you'll never get out of debt or that you can't afford to save or invest. To shift your mindset, start by believing that you can take control of your financial situation. Develop a debt repayment plan, this will make you see the light at the end of the tunnel, that is, it will give you a date as close as possible to the day you will get out of all your debts, and at the same time the day you will start saving to prepare for investments.

The optimist or the Investor: If you're an investor, you likely understand the value of using money to make more money. However, ensure your mindset isn't solely focused on making money without considering the potential risks. Balance is key. Diversify your investments and ensure you have a solid financial base (like an emergency fund and insurance) before taking on higher-risk investments.

The Avoider: If you're an avoider, you might believe that money is a source of stress or confusion. To shift your mindset, start by believing that you can understand and manage your finances effectively. Educate yourself about personal finance, start tracking your income and expenses, and engage in financial planning.

Your way of thinking is the driving force behind your financial decisions. It is the lens through which you view money and wealth. It influences how you save, how you spend, and how you invest. In short, the way you think shapes your financial reality. But how do we change a mindset that's been ingrained in us since childhood? How do we make these changes happen within ourselves?

Fortunately, our mindset, much like any other skill, can be honed and redirected towards achieving different objectives. The process, while simple, requires discipline and commitment.

If you were advising a young man aspiring to be the best pianist, you'd likely suggest he seek a tutor, learn continuously, and practice diligently. The same principle applies here. To shift your mindset towards wealth accumulation, you need to learn every day, apply your newfound knowledge, and seek professional advice when necessary.

Let's delve into the strategies that will guide you in shifting your mindset towards wealth accumulation:

Embrace Learning: The first step towards shifting your mindset is embracing learning. Knowledge is power, especially when it comes to personal finance. The more you understand about money management, investing, and wealth accumulation, the better equipped you'll be to make informed decisions. Make it a habit to learn something new about finances every day. This could be reading a chapter of a financial book, listening to a finance podcast, or even attending a seminar or workshop. As you learn, you'll start to see money in a new light - not as a source of stress or confusion, but as a tool that you can use to build wealth and achieve financial freedom.

Challenge Your Beliefs: Reflect on your existing beliefs about money. Are they helping you or hindering you? If you find that you're harboring negative beliefs, consciously work on replacing them with positive ones. For instance, instead of thinking 'I'll never be wealthy', affirm 'I have the power to accumulate wealth'.

Embrace Positive Behaviors: Identify the behaviors that contribute to wealth accumulation, such as saving, investing, and mindful spending. Make a deliberate effort to integrate these behaviors into your daily life. If you're a spender, this might mean setting a budget for discretionary spending. If you're a saver, it might mean learning about investing to grow your wealth.

Learn from the Successful: Seek inspiration from successful wealth accumulators. What habits and attitudes do they possess that you can emulate? Learn from their triumphs and their missteps. Reading books, listening to podcasts, or following blogs about personal finance can provide valuable insights.

Set Financial Goals: Clear, achievable financial goals can motivate you to change your habits and stay on track. Whether it's saving for a down payment, paying off debt, or investing for retirement, having a goal provides a tangible target to strive for.

Practice Gratitude: Instead of focusing on what you lack, concentrate on what you have. Practicing gratitude can shift your mindset from scarcity to abundance, which is key to wealth accumulation. Start a gratitude journal or make it a daily habit to list three things you're grateful for.

Changing one's mindset is not a one-time event, but rather a journey of growth, learning, and constant adaptation. It requires patience, commitment, and resilience; you are making a powerful statement to yourself - that you are capable of, and committed to, becoming a successful wealth hoarder.

In the end, the power to transform your financial future lies in your hands.

You have the ability to rewrite your financial narrative, one mindset shift at a time. So, begin today and unlock the power of a positive money mindset for wealth accumulation. You're more capable than you believe, and the wealth you aspire to accumulate is within your reach. Remember, every day is a chance to take another step towards your financial prosperity. Keep going, and never stop evolving.

Reflection Questions/Exercises

Identify and Transform: Start by identifying a limiting belief you have about money. It could be something like "I can never save enough" or "Investing is too risky for me." Write it down in your notebook or journal. Now think of a positive, empowering belief to replace it. For example, if your limiting belief is "I will never be able to save enough," you could replace it with "I am capable of saving consistently and increasing my wealth over time." Make a commitment to remind yourself of this new belief every day for a week.

Long-term vision: Create a simple but powerful financial goal that represents a long-term vision, an ultimate goal. It could be something like "I want to own 300 real estate properties" or "I want to retire with $10 Million in investments." Write it in your notebook or journal, we will use it later. Having a tangible goal will keep you focused on your wealth accumulation journey.

Think of a person in your life whom you consider financially successful and as having a wealthy mindset. Write down their name. Reflect on their financial habits, attitudes, and behaviors. What characteristics do they have that align with a wealth accumulator's mindset? This could be things like disciplined saving, strategic investing, continuous learning about finance, or a positive attitude towards money. Write down these characteristics, and for each one, explain why you think this person embodies that trait. What actions or attitudes have you observed that support your belief?

Evaluating Your Financial Mindset: Strengths and Weaknesses Exercise

For this exercise, you'll be identifying your financial strengths and weaknesses to understand better where you stand currently with your wealth accumulator's mindset.

Identify Your Strengths: Reflect on your positive financial habits and attitudes. This could be anything from consistently saving a portion of your income, not being impulsive with money, having a good understanding of basic financial concepts, or being comfortable with discussing finances. Write down at least three financial strengths you possess.

Identify Your Weaknesses: Reflect on areas where you feel you struggle financially. This could be anything from difficulty sticking to a budget, not being aware of where your money goes, lacking knowledge about investing, or having a mindset that believes you'll never be wealthy. Write down at least three financial weaknesses or areas for improvement.

Formulate Action Steps: For each weakness identified, write down at least one action step you can take to improve in that area. If you struggle with budgeting, for example, your action step could be to start tracking your expenses and create a realistic budget.

This exercise will not only help you understand your current mindset towards finances but also provide you with clear action steps to start improving in the areas where you're weak.

Setting Your Wealth Accumulation Goals

If you have come this far with me, you have proven yourself an exceptional reader and a proactive learner. I trust you've diligently completed the exercises and tasks outlined thus far: you've carefully crafted your Financial Snapshot, you've unearthed your 'money personality', and you've evaluated your financial mindset strengths and weaknesses. Congratulations! You're armed with critical self-knowledge that will help you refine or redefine your financial goals for the short, medium, and long term.

We all have aspirations, but often, these are born from a comfort zone built on familiar knowledge and societal expectations. For instance, many view homeownership as a mandatory step on the road to success—it's a commonly touted ambition. However, from a financial perspective, this goal may not always be the most beneficial. A house, while offering security and comfort, often presents a significant liability that could drain your resources and even lead to financial distress in worst-case scenarios.

Recognizing this dichotomy is why learning to establish informed financial goals is so essential. It allows you to decipher which ambitions will genuinely lead you closer to financial freedom.

Setting clear and realistic wealth accumulation goals is a critical step on your journey to financial prosperity. These goals serve as your financial compass, guiding your decisions and actions. They provide a sense of direction and purpose, keeping you focused and motivated even when the journey gets tough.

Imagine embarking on a road trip without a final destination in mind. You might enjoy the ride for a while, but eventually, you'll start to feel lost and aimless. The same principle applies to your financial journey. Without clear goals that add value to your finances, you might find yourself drifting aimlessly, making impulsive decisions that hinder your wealth accumulation efforts.

Let's understand the difference between assets and liabilities in the context of wealth accumulation. The simplest way to distinguish them is: an asset puts money into your pocket, whereas a liability takes money out of your pocket.

An asset can be a property you rent out, dividends from shares you own, or interest from your savings or a business you own. A liability, on the other hand, includes your mortgage, car payments, and credit card debts. These are expenses that, while necessary, drain resources that could otherwise be invested.

A common misunderstanding is that all property, like the house you live in, is an asset. While it may appreciate over time, if it's draining your finances through mortgage payments, maintenance, and taxes, then it is more of a liability. On the contrary, a property that you rent out that provides regular income is an asset.

But life is about more than just accumulating assets and avoiding liabilities— it's about finding a balance between the two. Let's dive into how you can strike that balance in your life.

We all need a place to live, a car for transportation, a cup of coffee to start the day and so on. However, there's a fine line between purchasing what you need and buying what you want. To maintain a balance, prioritize necessary liabilities and simultaneously contribute to your asset pool. This will likely require patience, budgeting, and occasionally, sacrifices.

The first step in purchasing necessary liabilities is to understand their true cost. For example, the real cost of owning a car isn't just the purchase price—it includes maintenance, fuel, insurance, and depreciation. By acknowledging these costs upfront, you can make a more informed decision about the necessity and affordability of the purchase.

It's tempting to match your lifestyle to your income, but this can lead to a trap of increasing liabilities. By living below your means, you'll have a surplus to invest in assets. This could mean choosing a smaller home, a used car over a new one or making your own cup of coffee at home—these decisions can significantly reduce your monthly liabilities.

Setting wealth accumulation goals isn't a one-size-fits-all approach. It's a deeply personal process that depends on your current financial snapshot, your risk tolerance, your life stage, and your future aspirations. The key is to start consciously setting goals that add financial value to your life, or at least setting goals that don't drain all your hard-earned money. Make or review your financial goals, are they helping you accumulate wealth or are they going to drain your economic power?

In order to paint a clearer picture, let's examine two distinct scenarios. These scenarios feature two individuals who share similar desires and end-goals. However, their approach towards achieving these goals differs significantly.

Person A - Wealth Financial Goals

Build an Emergency Fund: Save 6 months' worth of living expenses in a high-yield savings account within the next 18 months.

Pay Off Credit Card Debt: Eliminate $5000 in credit card debt within the next 12 months by making consistent monthly payments above the minimum due.

Invest in Retirement Funds: Max out contributions to 401(k) and Roth IRA accounts each year to take advantage of compound interest and tax benefits.

Invest in Income-Producing Assets: Purchase a rental property within the next 5 years to generate passive income.

Establish a Diversified Investment Portfolio: Allocate a certain percentage of monthly income to different investment tools (stocks, bonds, mutual funds) to ensure diversification and mitigate risk.

Increase Income Streams: Start a side business or freelance work within the next 2 years to create an additional income stream.

Buying a House: Rather than just purchasing a home based on desire, Person A does extensive research. They understand that a home is more of a liability than an asset, but also recognize the personal value in homeownership. They consider things like the potential for the home to appreciate, the cost of the mortgage versus renting, tax implications, the potential to rent out a portion of the home, and their long-term plans. They also ensure they have a 20% down payment saved to avoid extra costs like Private Mortgage Insurance (PMI).

Planning Vacations: Person A views vacations as an important part of life, for relaxation and creating memories. They plan and save for vacations in advance, making sure to budget for all costs (flights, accommodation, meals, activities, etc.) They avoid going into debt for vacations and take advantage of credit card points and off-peak travel to save money.

Person B - Unfamiliar with Wealth Accumulation

Save Money: Try to save some money each month without a clear goal or purpose.

Pay Off Debt: Attempt to reduce debt by making minimum payments on credit cards, without a defined timeline or strategy.

Retirement Planning: Have some money deducted for a retirement account without understanding the benefits of maxing out contributions or the power of compound interest.

Buy a House: Plan to buy a house because it seems like the right thing to do, without considering the financial implications or alternatives (like investing in income-producing properties).

Investing: Consider investing in stocks or mutual funds without a clear strategy or understanding of risk diversification.

Increase Earnings: Hope for a raise or promotion to increase income, without considering other potential income streams.

Buying a House: Person B decides they want to buy a house because it's "what you're supposed to do." They don't do extensive research on the financial implications or consider other options like renting or investing in rental properties. They may only save the minimum down payment, not realizing the extra costs they'll incur.

Planning Vacations: Person B plans vacations based on desire and often does not budget properly or save in advance. They may end up putting a lot of their trip expenses on credit cards without a clear plan for paying off the balance quickly. This approach can lead to accumulated debt and paying more for the vacation in the long run due to interest charges.

As you can see, both individuals can achieve lifestyle goals like homeownership or going on vacation, but the approach can greatly affect their financial health. A wealth accumulator, like Person A, approaches these goals with a strategic plan and an understanding of the financial implications, ensuring their lifestyle goals contribute to their financial health rather than detract from it.

By differentiating between assets and liabilities, understanding their impact on your financial health, and strategically managing your purchases, you can build a robust financial plan. This will not only help reduce your liabilities but also pave the way for consistent wealth accumulation.

Designing Your Budget

Budgeting is one of the most important skills in personal finance. It is the process of creating a plan for how you will spend your money, taking into account your income and expenses. Budgeting helps you to live within your means, avoid overspending, and make better financial decisions.

This map, or plan, shows you how to allocate your hard-earned money, taking into consideration your income and expenses. It's your personal guide to living within your means, dodging the trap of overspending, and making smarter decisions with your money.

A budget isn't just a suggestion, it's a critical step when starting to build wealth. Building wealth is a long-term game, one that requires commitment to saving and investing. Budgeting acts as your personal finance coach, helping you to prioritize your spending and allocate your resources in ways that align with your financial goals.

Without a budget, it's all too easy to slip into a pattern of overspending, living beyond your means, and ending up in a cycle of debt and financial stress. While there are m any budgeting strategies out there, one particular method stands out in its effectiveness - **Zero-Based Budgeting**.

A zero-based budget is a method where every dollar you earn has a role to play. Whether it's destined for a specific expense or set aside for a savings goal, each dollar is assigned a task. In this way, by the end of the month, you're left with no 'extra' money. Now, that doesn't mean you've spent all you've earned. Instead, it ensures that each dollar has been accounted for and used wisely.

Zero-based budgeting is an especially helpful tool when you're starting your wealth-building journey. It encourages you to critically examine your spending habits and align your expenses with your financial aspirations. By pinpointing areas where you can cut back on spending, you can free up funds to channel towards savings and investments.

It's important to understand that zero-based budgeting isn't about spending all you earn. Rather, it's about making sure each dollar counts. Without a clear budget, money sitting idle in your account can seem like 'extra' cash, a temptation for impulsive spending. Zero-based budgeting puts each dollar to work, ensuring that all your funds have a purpose and are actively contributing to your wealth accumulation goals. By putting your money to work in this way, you're effectively stepping away from the temptation of aimless spending and taking proactive strides towards your financial goals.

How to make the budget is one of the most frequent concerns, as we mentioned at the beginning of this chapter, so we are going to go step by step and how to create this budget and then we will see a final example of how your budget should look at the end of this exercise.

Steps to Creating a Zero-Based Budget

Identify Monthly Income: Include all your income sources, just like you did while creating your financial snapshot.

List All Expenses: Begin with necessary expenditures, like housing, utilities, food, transportation, etc., and then move to discretionary spending like entertainment or dining out. Remember to include occasional expenses like annual insurance premiums or car maintenance.

Assign Every Dollar: Once you've listed all your income and expenses, start allocating every dollar of your income to a category. This includes contributions to savings and investment accounts.

Track and Adjust: Throughout the month, keep track of your actual spending and compare it with your budget. If you find that you've over- or under-budgeted in some categories, adjust accordingly. Remember, a budget is a living document and needs tweaking from time to time.

here's a hypothetical example of a very simple zero-based budget for a family with a monthly income of $5000:

In this example, all the income for the month has been allocated to different expense categories and savings goals, and the 'Left to Budget' amount is zero, as it should be in a zero-based budget.

Category	Budgeted Amount
Income	$ 5000
Total Income	**$ 5000**
Expenses	
Housing (Mortgage/Rent)	$ 1500
Utilities (Electric, Water, Gas, Internet)	$ 300
Food (Groceries, Dining Out)	$ 600
Insurance (Health, Car, Home)	$ 400
Transportation (Gas, Car Maintenance)	$ 200
Education (School Supplies, Tuition)	$ 300
Pets (Food, Vet Visits)	$ 100
Entertainment (Subscriptions, Events)	$ 200
Miscellaneous	$ 100
Personal (Clothing, Personal Care)	$ 200
Health (Prescriptions, Doctor Visits)	$ 100
Savings/Investments	
Emergency Fund	$ 500
Retirement Account	$ 300
College Fund	$ 200
Total Expenses	**$ 5000**
Total Income - Expenses	**$ 0**

You can tailor your budget to your specific needs and preferences. By incorporating details like dates, categories, account names, and bank names, you can create a more comprehensive view. Design it in a way that provides clarity at a single glance. Let's dive into an example.

Here is another example of a more detailed version of the zero-based budget table:

Item	Category	Estimate	Actual Pay	Date	Total
Salary	Income	$ 5000	$ 5000	31/08/23	$ 5000
Mortgage	Housing	$ 1500	$ 1500	01/09/23	$ -1500
Electric Payment	Utilities	$ 100	$ 105	10/09/23	$ -105
Water Bill	Utilities	$ 75	$ 70	112/09/23	$ -70
Gas Bill	Utilities	$ 75	$ 80	20/09/23	$ -80
Internet	Utilities	$ 90	$ 91.99	21/09/23	$ -91.99
Groceries	Food	$ 400	$ 425	09/25/23	$ -425
Dining Out	Food	$ 200	$ 175	Month	$ -175
Health Insurance	Insurance	$ 200	$ 200	09/27/23	$ -200
Retirament Account	Invest	$ 300	$ 300	09/27/23	$ -300
Saving Account	Savings	$ 200	$ 200	09/28/23	$ -200

You would continue this table for every expense you have. At the end, the sum of your expenses should be equal to your income, i.e., 5000.

The 'Estimate' column contains your anticipated amounts for each item based on previous months' spending or fixed payment amounts. The 'Actual Payment' column shows what you actually end up spending or depositing. The 'Date' column shows when these transactions usually occur, and the 'Deposit to Account' column is where you record money that is being saved or invested.

Whether you choose to follow a simple system as shown in the first example or opt for a more detailed version like the second, the ultimate goal remains the same: understanding precisely where each hard-earned dollar is allocated. The level of detail in your budgeting comes down to personal preference and the complexity of your financial situation. The key here is to have a firm grasp on your spending limits for each category or specific item. This hands-on approach not only ensures that your money is being managed effectively but also promotes a heightened awareness and discipline in your spending habits. With every dollar assigned a purpose, you have a clear roadmap directing you towards your financial goals.

Exercise: Create Your Zero-Based Budget

Using the steps provided in the chapter, create your first zero-based budget. Start by listing all your income sources and expenses for the upcoming month. Assign every dollar of your income to a category. At the end of the month, compare your actual spending with your budgeted amounts. Were there any surprises? Did you need to adjust any categories?

Saving: The Foundation of Wealth

The first step in wealth accumulation is saving. The initial stride towards wealth accumulation begins with cultivating a habit of saving. This might seem like a basic concept, but it's a fundamental one that many people overlook. Saving is the act of setting aside a portion of your income for future use. It's the process of resisting immediate gratification in favor of long-term security.

Imagine you're building a house. Before you can even think about the walls or the roof, you need to lay a solid foundation. Without it, the house would crumble. The same principle applies to wealth accumulation. Before you can build wealth, you need to lay a solid foundation. And that foundation is saving.

Saving is more than just putting money aside. It's a mindset. It's about understanding that every dollar you save is a step towards your financial freedom. It's about making choices today that will benefit your future self.

But how do you save money? It's a question that seems simple, yet many of us struggle with it. The answer lies in understanding your income and expenses. It's about knowing where your money is going and making conscious decisions about what to do with it.

Let's say you're earning $4000 a month. After paying for your rent, groceries, utilities, and other necessities, you're left with $1000. What do you do with that money? Do you spend it on a new phone, a fancy dinner, or a pair of designer shoes? Or do you save it for your future?

The answer to that question is what separates spenders from savers. Spenders see that $1000 as an opportunity to buy something they want. Savers, on the other hand, see it as an opportunity to build their wealth.

Wealth accumulation begins with a single step; understanding where your money is going. It's a simple concept, yet one that many people overlook. After all, it's easy to swipe a card or click a button and not think about the money that's being spent. But those small, seemingly insignificant amounts can quickly add up, leaving you wondering where your paycheck went at the end of the month.

This is where the art of saving comes into play. It's not just about setting aside a portion of your income each month (although that's certainly important). It's about developing a deep, intimate understanding of your financial habits. It's about knowing where every cent of your hard-earned money is going and making conscious decisions about how to spend it.

Creating a monthly budget is key to mastering this art. A budget is more than just a financial tool; it's a reflection of your priorities and values. It allows you to take control of your money, rather than letting your money control you.

Now, let's get practical. How can you start saving money and paying off your debt? Here are a few exercises you can do:

Track your income and expenses: For one month, write down every dollar you earn and every dollar you spend. At the end of the month, analyze your spending habits. Are there areas where you can cut back?

Open a High-Yield Savings Account: Consider placing your savings in a high-yield savings account. These accounts offer interest rates significantly higher than regular savings accounts, allowing your money to grow faster. Remember, it's not just about saving; it's also about making your money work for you.

Pay Yourself First: As soon as you receive your paycheck, allocate a certain portion to your savings. Treat it as a necessary expenditure, just like rent or utilities.

Set Up Automatic Transfers: Use your bank's services to automatically transfer a specified amount from your checking account to your high-yield savings account each month. This way, the savings happen seamlessly, reducing the temptation to spend.

Reduce Unnecessary Expenses: Identify and cut down on non-essential expenditures. Whether it's dining out less often, canceling unused subscriptions, or switching to a cheaper grocery store, small savings can add up over time.

Implement a Cooling-off Period: Wait for 24-48 hours before making any impulse purchases. This period gives you time to reconsider and often saves you from spending on items you don't truly need.

Prepare Meals at Home: Frequently eating out can be a major drain on your budget. Preparing meals at home is a cost-effective and healthier alternative.

Develop a debt repayment plan: If you have debt, create a plan to pay it off. Prioritize high-interest debt, as it's the most costly.

Saving is the bedrock of wealth accumulation. It's not just about hoarding money; it's about creating the financial freedom to make choices that can grow your wealth. The methods discussed in this section – from opening a high-yield savings account to spending wisely and embracing frugal habits – are but a few of the numerous strategies to start saving now.

But remember, we don't save just for the sake of saving. We save to accumulate a substantial financial reserve that gives us the power to invest and put our hard-earned money to work.

Exercise: Reflect on the budget you created in the previous exercise.

Do you have a designated category for savings?

If yes, evaluate the amount allocated. Do you believe this amount is sufficient to meet your short-term and long-term financial goals?
If not, consider why you have not allocated funds for savings. Is it due to a lack of funds, prioritizing other expenses, or some other reason?

Be sure to write your answers and reflections in your notebook or financial journal. This exercise will not only provide insights into your current financial habits but also highlight areas that need improvement for successful wealth accumulation.

Investing: The Catalyst for Growth

While saving provides the foundation for wealth accumulation, investing is the catalyst that accelerates its growth. Investing involves committing your money to ventures that have the potential to generate returns. This could be in the form of stocks, bonds, mutual funds, real estate, or even a small business.

Investing is like planting a seed and nurturing while you wait for it to grow. The seed is your initial investment, and the nurturing involves monitoring your investments, making adjustments as necessary, and being patient as your wealth grows over time.

For instance, if you invest your $10 savings in a venture that generates a 10% annual return, you'll have $11 at the end of the year. If you reinvest the $11, it will grow to about $12.10 by the end of the second year. This process, known as compounding, is one of the most powerful wealth-building tools at your disposal.

However, it's important to note that investing should only begin once you have a solid financial foundation. This means having no high-interest debts and having a good emergency fund in place. High-interest debts can eat away at your potential investment returns, and without an emergency fund, you might be forced to sell your investments if an unexpected expense arises.

Let's take a journey into the world of investing, exploring the different paths you can take to grow your wealth. Each path has its own unique landscape, filled with opportunities and challenges. As we journey through, remember that the best path for you depends on your personal financial goals, risk tolerance, and investment horizon.

Stock Market: Picture yourself as part owner of a thriving company, sharing in its successes. That's what investing in the stock market is like. When you buy shares of a company, you're buying a piece of that company. As the company grows and profits, the value of your shares increases, a phenomenon known as capital appreciation. Some companies even share a portion of their profits with shareholders through dividends.

For example, if you had invested $1,000 in Amazon when it first went public in 1997, your investment would be worth over a million dollars today! However, the stock market is not without its risks. Prices can fluctuate, and companies can underperform. It's crucial to research and understand the companies you invest in and consider diversifying your portfolio to spread the risk.

Real Estate: Imagine owning a piece of land or a building, watching its value increase over time, and even earning regular income from it. That's the essence of real estate investing. You could invest in residential properties (like houses or apartments), commercial properties (like office buildings or shopping centers), or rental properties.

Consider the story of a couple who bought a small apartment building in a growing city. They rented out the apartments, earning a steady stream of income. Over time, as the city grew and property values increased, so did the value of their buildings. However, real estate investing requires significant upfront capital and ongoing management. It's not for the faint of heart, but the rewards can be substantial.

Business Investment: Now, envision yourself as a silent partner in a promising startup, helping it grow and sharing in its profits. That's what investing in a small business looks like. As an investor, you provide capital to help the business grow. In return, you get a share of the profits.

Take the example of an early investor in Uber. Despite the risks and the company's initial lack of profits, they saw potential in the business model and invested. When Uber went public in 2019, early investors saw significant returns on their investment. However, investing in small businesses is risky. Many fails within the first few years. It's vital to thoroughly evaluate the business plan, understand the market, and assess the competence of the management team before investing.

Building a Small Business: Picture yourself at the helm of your own enterprise, steering it towards growth and profitability. That's what building a small business entails. As a business owner, you're not just investing your money; you're also investing your time, skills, and effort.

Building a small business can be a rewarding journey, but it's also fraught with challenges. It requires a viable business idea, a well-crafted business plan, a great team, and the tenacity to overcome obstacles. You'll need to wear many hats, from product development and marketing to sales and customer service.

But the potential rewards are significant. Not only can a successful business provide a steady stream of income, but it can also increase in value over time, leading to substantial wealth accumulation. Plus, there's the satisfaction of knowing that you've created something valuable, not just for yourself, but for your employees and customers as well.

However, it's important to note that building a business also involves risk. Many businesses fail within the first few years. It's crucial to thoroughly evaluate your business idea, understand your market, and have a solid plan in place before you start. And remember, it's okay to start small. Many successful businesses started as side hustles or small projects. The key is to start, learn, and grow.

Each of these investment avenues has its own set of risks and rewards. The real key is to choose the ones that are align with your financial goals, risk tolerance, and time horizon. Remember, the goal of investing is not to get rich quick, but to grow your wealth steadily over time.

In addressing the question of how to begin investing, the path you choose must be tailored to your unique financial situation, goals, and in consultation with a professional financial advisor. No two situations are identical, and therefore, there's no one-size-fits-all solution to this question.

Pay close attention to this critical point: Prior to dipping your toes into any investment, prioritize education. As highlighted in the earlier sections of this book, financial literacy is not merely beneficial—it's essential. Just as you're shaping your financial path, initiate your journey of financial learning concurrently.

Does this mean you will need professional assistance? Absolutely. I strongly recommend that you seek as much professional guidance as needed. However, the knowledge and insight you acquire independently will magnify the value you derive from a professional's advice. Equipped with your own understanding, you'll be able to engage more effectively, ask more informed questions, and make decisions that truly align with your financial aspirations. So, while experts can provide guidance, it's your informed participation that's the key to successful investing.

Balancing Saving and Investing

While both saving and investing are crucial for wealth accumulation, it's important to strike a balance between the two. Saving provides financial security and prepares you for unexpected expenses, while investing propels your wealth growth.

A good rule of thumb is to first build an emergency fund through savings. This fund should cover three to six months' worth of living expenses. Once you have a solid emergency fund, you can start channeling more of your income towards investments.

Regardless of whether you choose to invest in the stock market, your own business, or real estate, the priority should be to begin investing only after establishing a robust savings cushion. This saved amount should remain separate from your investment capital, ideally kept in a liquid account that ensures quick access during emergencies. Such a financial buffer ensures that even if your investments don't yield the anticipated returns, you aren't left empty-handed. This approach not only provides security but also instills confidence when diving into investment opportunities.

Balancing savings and investments can be best achieved by aligning them with your goals, both short-term and long-term. Recognizing the significance of these goals, we've addressed them prior to discussing the budget in this chapter. These goals, while potentially evolving over time, act as your compass, directing how you allocate resources between saving and investing. This way, you can make decisions that resonate with your personal aspirations and comfort levels. Whether you're setting money aside for a much-anticipated family vacation next summer or investing for a serene retirement two decades down the road, a clear understanding of your goals helps in decision-making. However, remember that life's paths are rarely linear. Periodically re-evaluate your financial strategies, and be ready to adjust if circumstances dictate.

It requires patience, discipline, and a well-thought-out strategy. By understanding the role of saving and investing, you can navigate this journey more effectively and build a financial future that aligns with your dreams and aspirations.

The Power of Compound Interest

The magic of wealth accumulation lies not in the grandeur of a single, monumental financial decision, but in the quiet consistency of small, calculated actions repeated over time. This is the essence of compound interest, a fundamental principle that has been aptly described as the eighth wonder of the world by none other than Albert Einstein himself.

Compound interest is the process by which the interest you earn on your savings or investments is added to your original amount, forming a larger base on which future interest is calculated. This cycle, repeated over time, can lead to exponential growth of your wealth. It's like a snowball rolling down a hill, gathering more snow and momentum as it goes along.

To illustrate, let's consider a simple example. Suppose you invest $1,000 at an annual interest rate of 5%. After the first year, you'll earn $50 in interest, bringing your total to $1,050. In the second year, you'll earn interest not just on your initial $1,000, but also on the $50 interest from the first year. So, your interest for the second year would be $52.50, and your total would rise to $1,102.50. This process continues year after year, with each year's interest being calculated on an ever-increasing amount.

Now, let's consider the real-world implications of this principle. Imagine a young professional, let's call her Lisa, who starts contributing to her 401(k) at the age of 25. She contributes $200 every month, and her investments earn an average annual return of 7%. By the time Lisa retires at 65, she would have contributed a total of $96,000. However, thanks to the power of compound interest, her 401(k) balance would have grown to over $525,000!

The principle of compound interest applies not just to traditional investments like stocks and bonds, but also to other forms of wealth accumulation such as real estate and small businesses. Whether it's the appreciation of property value over time, the growth of business revenue, or the reinvestment of profits, the underlying mechanism is the same. It's all about letting your money work for you, growing and multiplying over time.

So, how can you harness the power of compound interest to accumulate wealth? Here are a few strategies:

Start Early: The earlier you start saving and investing, more time your money has to grow. Even small amounts can add up to significant sums over time.

Save Regularly: Make saving and investing a regular habit. Whether it's a fixed amount every month or a percentage of your income, consistency is key.

Reinvest Your Returns: Don't just spend the interest or returns you earn. Reinvest them to further boost your wealth accumulation.

Be Patient: Compound interest is a long-term game. Don't be discouraged if you don't see substantial growth in the initial years. Remember, the most significant growth happens in the later years due to the snowball effect.

Avoid High-Interest Debt: High-interest and bad debt can eat away at your savings and returns, negating the effects of compound interest. Try to pay off such debts as soon as possible.

The power of compound interest is not just a financial concept; it's a philosophy of patience, consistency, and long-term thinking. It's about understanding that wealth accumulation is not a sprint, but a marathon. It's about realizing that the small, seemingly insignificant actions you take today can have a profound impact on your financial future.

As you navigate your journey towards wealth accumulation, let the power of compound interest be your guiding star. Embrace it, harness it, and watch as it transforms your financial landscape, one compounded interest at a time.

Cultivating Financial Resilience

Financial resilience is the ability to weather financial shocks and recover quickly from financial misfortunes. It is a critical determinant of lasting financial prosperity.

Resilience, in general terms, refers to the capacity of an individual to deal with a disruptive event or adversity, resist its immediate impact, and recover over time. It's essentially about being able to bounce back from difficulties and setbacks and adapt to change.

When you're on the path to wealth accumulation, it's important to recognize the role of financial resilience. Your goal is not just to earn money, but to protect it and make it grow, even in the face of challenges. Financial resilience gives you the flexibility to adapt to changes in your financial landscape, such as a sudden job loss, a medical emergency or a market downturn or any other unforeseen event.

There are a number of things you can do to build financial resilience. First of all, you must establish an emergency fund, as we have told you before, from 3 to 6 months of monthly expenses, it could even be a little more, as far as you feel comfortable. This cash reserve that is earmarked specifically for unexpected expenses can help you avoid having to resort to credit or withdraw early from long-term investments when unexpected expenses arise.

Another important way to build financial resilience is to get insurance. Insurance can help protect you from unexpected substantial expenses, such as medical bills, car repairs, or property damage. There are many different types of insurance available, so you can choose the ones that best suit your needs.

Diversifying your income is another way to increase financial resilience.

This means having multiple streams of income so that if one source dries up, you have others to rely on. You can diversify your income by starting a side business, investing in real estate, or creating passive income streams through online businesses, although I make it very clear again that before you put your money and time into any type of investment you must have a good emergency fund.

It is important to stay up to date on financial matters. One more time, until you get tired of hearing it, it is important to be aware of the latest trends and developments in the world of finance. You should stay informed by reading books and articles, attending workshops, or consulting with a financial advisor. Constant learning is the only thing that will arm you with powerful tools to grow your wealth.

Cultivating financial resilience is an ongoing process. It requires regular reassessment and adjustments of your financial strategy, along with an unwavering dedication to lifelong learning.

Exercise:

Take some time to brainstorm and write down a list of 10 strategies or activities you could undertake in the next year to boost your financial literacy and resilience. These can range from reading books about finance, attending webinars, courses or seminars, seeking professional financial advice, to implementing practical money-management habits.

Remember, the goal of this exercise is to encourage you to become more proactive and conscious about your finances. Write down your list in your notebook or financial journal and make sure to revisit it periodically to check your progress.

CHAPTER 4

Prosperity Pursuit

Take ACTION

"Don't put off till tomorrow what you can do today," Benjamin Franklin once said, and I absolutely adore this phrase. It encapsulates the essence of seizing the day, of taking life by the horns, and of jumping at opportunities when they present themselves. And this, dear reader, is precisely what this chapter is about—moving from thought to action, from knowledge to practice, and from contemplation to actualization.

You have equipped yourself with valuable knowledge, amassed wisdom, and hopefully cultivated a renewed mindset throughout the previous chapters. But as we have discussed, acquiring knowledge is only half the battle. The true test lies in the application of that knowledge. Can we translate our plans into action? Can we embody the principles we've learned? Can we convert our newfound financial understanding into tangible results?

The key to reshaping our future lies in our hands, and the power to change our financial narrative begins with action. Do you truly yearn for a better, more secure future for yourself and your family? Well, if the answer is a resounding 'yes,' then the moment to act is not tomorrow or the day after; it is now.

Each day we have the opportunity to act is a gift. Each moment is a chance to make decisions that can change our financial trajectory. Every choice to save rather than spend, to invest rather than squander, reflects the lessons we've learned.

This chapter is all about urging you into motion. It is about taking all those lessons about goals, mindset, budgeting, debt, savings, investment, and resilience, and bringing them to life. It is about understanding that today's actions will be the reflection of tomorrow's reality.

Our future prosperity depends on our ability to pursue it with determination, with passion, and above all, with action. This chapter, then, is the beginning of your pursuit of prosperity. Let's journey together into transforming knowledge into action, as we move forward on this path to financial freedom and wealth accumulation. Today's actions will set the course for a financially prosperous tomorrow.

Step 1: Translating Goals into Actions

Ah, the pivotal power of goals. Goals are not just wishes we hope will come true, nor are they abstract ideas floating aimlessly in our minds. Goals are powerful tools for transforming your vision into reality. The journey to wealth accumulation isn't a casual stroll in the park; it requires determination, persistence, and above all, an unwavering dedication to change.

The art of change lies in reinvention. You must adopt new habits, embrace new perspectives, and stoke the fire of self-motivation. The reality is, what you've been doing up until this point has brought you here, but if you want to experience a different financial reality, you need to do something differently. Accumulating wealth isn't an overnight phenomenon. It's not about instant gratification, but rather a gradual, consistent transformation over time.

You didn't believe that merely reading a book would make you rich overnight, did you? Indeed, I'm a strong advocate for continuous learning. Opening your mind to new concepts and ideas is crucial. However, learning is just one part of the equation; the other part is putting this learning into action. And the fuel that powers this action is motivation—a deep, intrinsic motivation rooted in powerful motives that keep you pushing forward, even when the going gets tough.

This motivation comes from your goals—goals that are so compelling that they can energize you for the next 10, 20 years, or even a lifetime. Your goals are your 'why.' They are the reason you wake up every morning and strive for financial freedom. So, let's start with a simple yet powerful exercise—rewriting your personal goals.

Today is the day to take action. So, grab that notebook or journal, which we've been using since the beginning and that you'll dedicate to this journey of wealth building over the next two decades. Write down your most important goals, the reasons why you're on this journey. Limit them to 3 or 4 maximum. You might think that's not enough. You might feel you have many more goals. But I assure you, many of your goals can be summarized in a few powerful sentences. The key here is to articulate a goal so potent that it continually propels you forward, even when the road seems long and challenging.

Once you've outlined your major goals, the next step is to deconstruct them into smaller, achievable objectives, each with a clear timeline. For instance, if your primary goal is to "Own my dream home, financed by the income generated from my other properties and my investments," you can break this down into manageable steps like "Save $X for a down payment within the next 3 months," or "Purchase my first rental property within the year." Feel free to fragment these into as many mini-goals as you need, but ensure each has a realistic and specific timeline. These micro-goals are designed for you to achieve with relative ease over time, serving as motivational milestones along your journey. Each achieved goal will imbue you with a sense of accomplishment and propel you to reach further.

Remember, the journey to wealth accumulation is about progress, not perfection. It's about taking one step at a time, and these smaller goals will help guide your steps.

Step 2: Cultivating the Wealth Accumulator's Mindset

As Gautama Buddha wisely said, 'The mind is everything. What you think, you become.' As mentioned in our workshop chapter, our thoughts and beliefs dictate our actions, which in turn, carve out our reality. That's why the nurturing of a wealth accumulator's mindset is an integral milestone in our action plan. It's not just a step—it's a pledge you make to yourself to foster a mindset of abundance and wealth throughout this journey and beyond.

You already possess the knowledge needed to foster this mindset. However, this chapter is about rolling up your sleeves and getting down to business. So, let's venture on this second step (the first being getting this book, got you!), and persist in fostering the mindset that will make you not just wealthier, but more deserving of wealth.

The first task is to earmark time in your schedule for one or more activities mentioned in the workshop, designed to foster your wealth accumulator's mindset. Remember our discussion around Embracing Learning, Challenging Your Beliefs, Adopting Positive Behaviors, Learning from Successful People, and Practicing Gratitude?—each of these activities should find a place in your daily routine, a ritual that continues for the rest of your life.

Commit to allocating necessary time for these activities, treating them as pivotal parts, as high-priority segments of your daily routine. Adjust your schedule to accommodate at least one activity each day. You could vary the activity daily, but the key is to dedicate a minimum of 30 minutes each day to cultivate and expand your wealth mindset.

When you write it down in your schedule, you lend authority to the activity. Instead of vaguely noting down '30 minutes of reading', specify what you plan to delve into. For instance, you could write '30 minutes of reading "Think and Grow Rich" by Napoleon Hill'. No need to break your bank—there's a goldmine of free resources at your disposal. Hunt for books, podcasts, guides, blogs, ebooks. Compile a list of books you're eager to read. Connect with entrepreneurs or professional networks and organize weekly gatherings. Search for these groups within your local vicinity—I guarantee they're out there. Remember, this is about taking action, so do it right now. Write everything down, create a list of possible activities, schedule them, and commit to carrying them out.

Make a 'Gratitude List' that lists all the things you appreciate and make it a constant companion to read aloud every day. Set a daily reminder on your phone to review this list and soak up the positivity it offers. Feel free to add to the list with new entries daily or weekly, as you discover more things in your life to be grateful for. However, don't stay a passive reader, take action now! Take your phone and create that reminder now.

Scan your network and identify the people in your circle that are in your belief more successful than you. Arrange a call to discuss your aspirations as a wealth accumulator, listen to their ideas, possibly this is the first step to scheduling an appointment to meet in person to learn more about your path to success. Who knows, they might connect you with even more successful people who can bring you further enrichment. That is what it means to take action.

Remember, your new mindset will guide you closer to your goals, but this mental shift will only occur through consistent action. The potency of the mind isn't about obsessing over something 24/7. True mental power lies in focusing on what truly matters and creating the necessary opportunities to achieve those objectives. Your mind is the soil; your actions, the seeds. Let's start planting.

Step 3: Redefining Your Budget

Reviewing your budget is an opportunity, not an inconvenience," It's a chance to examine your financial habits, identify opportunities for improvement, and put your money to work for you rather than the other way around. Your budget is your financial compass—it guides your financial decisions and ultimately steers you toward your wealth accumulation goals. So, let's use this moment to take a hard look at that budget of yours, not with judgment, but with a genuine desire to maximize its potential. Are you ready to take action?

Remember the budgeting exercise from the **"Wealth Wisdom Workshop"** chapter? I want you to pull out that budget now. Take a close look at it. Are there areas where you feel you can trim expenses? Is your money being allocated in a way that truly reflects your wealth accumulation goals? If your answer is 'no' to any of these questions, then it's time to redefine your budget. And you can do it right here, right now.

Reach for that trusty notebook once again and begin to meticulously revamp your budget. Show a firm commitment to financial optimization by pruning any unused subscriptions, streamlining your phone bill, and shopping around for more affordable car insurance. Make it a mission to ensure that every single penny is well allocated in this refreshed budget.

Redefining your budget isn't about slashing your expenses to the bone or living a barebones existence. It's about making thoughtful, purposeful decisions with your money. It's about aligning your budget with your wealth accumulation goals. This simple action—replanning your monthly budget—is a crucial first step in freeing up money from non-essential areas and redirecting it to where it will provide the most long-term benefit.

Let's consider an example. Suppose you discover that you're spending a significant portion of your income on dining out and entertainment. Analyzing your budget, you find that you spend $500 per month on these luxuries. By cutting this expenditure in half—eating at home more often or opting for less expensive forms of entertainment—you could save $250 each month.

This might not sound like much but consider this: if you invest this

$250 each month in a mutual fund with an average annual return of 7%, you'd accumulate over $113,000 in 20 years. This is the magic of compound interest, and it demonstrates the powerful impact of even small adjustments to your budget.

But let's dive deeper. Look at each line of your budget. Do you really need that expensive cable package, or could you switch to a cheaper streaming service? Are you spending too much on utilities? Maybe you can save by turning off lights when you leave the room, unplugging electronics, or adjusting your thermostat. Are you paying high fees on your bank account or credit card? Perhaps it's time to shop around for a better deal.

In every area of your budget, challenge yourself to find ways to save. Be creative, be bold, but also be realistic. Don't cut so much that you feel deprived or stressed. Remember, the goal is sustainable change, not quick fixes.

Once you've identified these savings, it's time to put that money to work. Don't just leave it sitting in your checking account, where it can be easily spent. Instead, create a new line in your budget for "Wealth Building." This could include additional contributions to your savings account, paying down debt more quickly, investing in the stock market, or saving for a down payment on a rental property.

The purpose of redefining your budget isn't just to save money—it's to use that money to generate more wealth, to start your emergency fund if you don't have one yet, to start saving money to invest in the future. It's about changing your perspective on budgeting, from viewing it as a tool to limit your spending to seeing it as a weapon to build your wealth.

Taking action now to redefine your budget could be the most powerful step you take towards your prosperity pursuit. And this action begins with being honest with yourself about your current spending habits and your willingness to change them. Your future self will thank you.

Step 4: Making Investment Decisions

Having arrived at this stage in your prosperity pursuit, you're equipped with a newfound financial acumen, a clear vision of your financial goals, and a solid foundation built upon a well-structured budget and judicious savings. This is a moment of celebration, but it's also a time for preparation. As we transition from saving to investing, we embark on a journey filled with excitement, opportunity, and responsibility.

Remember, before plunging into the world of investing, your financial foundation needs to be robust. If you've been diligently following along, by now, you've curbed high-interest debts, and a well-padded emergency fund is ready to catch you in case of unforeseen circumstances. Now, with this financial stability in place, we're ready to move forward. Let's delve deeper into making investing decisions.

Our previous discussions have exposed you to various forms of investments – stocks, bonds, real estate, mutual funds, and even starting your own business. Each of these opportunities carries its own set of risks and rewards. While variety is the spice of life, it is also the cornerstone of a healthy investment portfolio. The key to mitigating risk lies in diversification. By spreading your investments across a spectrum of asset classes, you're not just banking on one horse to win the race.

Now, an essential point I want to emphasize is the importance of prioritizing your retirement investment. No matter the number of goals you have on your list, securing your financial independence for the golden years of your life should be at the forefront. As a diligent saver and a mindful spender, you now have spare money in your budget. A good chunk of this should find its way into your retirement investment account.

The rest of your disposable income can fuel your other investment goals. Maybe you want to dip your toes into the real estate market? Or perhaps the entrepreneurial spark within you is yearning to kindle a business venture? Whatever it may be, you are now in control of your financial destiny. You have the freedom to allocate your money to accumulate wealth and amplify your prosperity.

As you navigate through the vast investment landscape, remember to seek professional guidance, that's the real and right call to action at this point. While this book has equipped you with the knowledge and mindset to make wise financial decisions, the complexities of the financial markets call for specialized expertise. A financial advisor can be your trusted companion on this journey, shedding light on intricate financial matters and helping you craft an investment strategy that aligns with your financial goals.

As we step into the world of investing, it's important to remember that this journey, like wealth accumulation, is a marathon, not a sprint. Each decision, each investment, takes you one step closer to your financial dreams. But the journey doesn't end here. You must continue to feed your knowledge and sharpen your mindset to handle the greater wealth that comes with wise investing.

You've come a long way since the beginning of this journey, and now you stand at the precipice of a new chapter. You are ready to transition from a diligent saver to a wise investor. This is not the end; it's the beginning of your wealth accumulation journey. Take a deep breath, brace yourself, and take the leap. The world of investing awaits you.

Step 5: Reviewing and Adjusting Your Financial Plan

Welcome to the final stride in our prosperity pursuit: the practice of constant evaluation and refinement. In the race to accumulate wealth, the finish line keeps moving forward as our ambitions grow, our circumstances change, and opportunities evolve. You've come far in your journey, steadily gathering the wisdom and experience of a proficient wealth accumulator. Now, it's time to apply this expertise to keep your financial plan agile and aligned with your evolving goals and changing life scenarios.

In life, change is the only constant. The dreams we once held close to our heart may seem distant or obsolete. Similarly, our financial goals also evolve. The once desired sports car may give way to the dream of owning a house or funding our children's education. Such changes require us to continually review and adapt our financial strategies.

There will be times when unexpected events or shifts in personal priorities necessitate a change in your financial strategy. Recognizing these moments and knowing how to pivot effectively is a critical aspect of financial resilience.

But, 'when' to pivot. Ideally, you should conduct a thorough review of your financial plan at least once or twice a year. However, life does not adhere to a schedule. Sometimes, dramatic changes occur that require immediate action: a job loss, a significant increase in income, an unexpected inheritance, or the onset of a global pandemic. When such events occur, it's time to revisit your financial plan and consider a pivot.

One of the most powerful traits of a successful wealth accumulator is adaptability. The ability to adjust your plans according to the changes in your life and the economy is a true hallmark of financial wisdom. With the solid financial foundation you've built along with the solid wealth accumulation skills you've honed; you now possess the tools to navigate this ongoing process.

Consider the financial plan as your compass. It guides you towards your financial north star. But as you traverse through the journey of life, the north star might shift. You might reach some goals sooner than you thought, new goals might spring up, or existing ones might lose their sheen. When such changes occur, it's time to recalibrate your compass – review your financial plan.

Reviewing your financial plan involves re-evaluating your budget, assessing the performance of your investments, and ensuring your plan aligns with your current financial goals. Have your monthly expenses increased? Have your sources of income diversified? How are your investments performing? Is your emergency fund robust enough to handle your current lifestyle? Is your retirement fund growing as planned? Questions like this help you evaluate where you stand.

Once you've reviewed your plan, you might find that adjustments are needed. Perhaps, you need to allocate more to your retirement savings or rebalance your investment portfolio. Maybe it's time to cut down on certain expenses or look for additional income streams.

At this stage, wealth accumulation has become a part of your identity. You've developed an instinct for financial opportunities, for identifying potential investments, and for opening new income channels. You've grown - both in wealth and in financial acumen. When you look at your growing emergency fund and your stress-free financial life, you see the tangible fruits of your efforts.

As your wealth grows, managing it becomes increasingly complex. Financial advisors can offer valuable information and personalized advice to optimize the growth of your wealth. At this point, enlisting the expertise of financial advisors can prove invaluable. These professionals can provide you with bespoke strategies and informed advice to enhance and optimize your wealth growth further.

At this stage, having successfully allocated a significant portion of your savings into productive investments, you'll find your financial journey enriched by an expanding network of skilled professionals. This network, your financial team, now includes accountants, lawyers, bankers, and stock investment advisors. You may even have found mentors whose advice and experiences guide your wealth accumulation journey.

Each member of this financial team brings their unique expertise to your aid. They can demystify the complexities of tax laws, guide you in selecting the most advantageous investment vehicles, and assist you in curating a balanced investment portfolio. This portfolio will be tailored specifically to your risk tolerance and financial objectives, ensuring your investments continue to serve your wealth accumulation ambitions effectively.

Your finance team is more than a group of professionals who assist you. They become part of your wealth accumulation journey, contributing their knowledge and experience to your growing financial acumen. Take advantage of their skills, consulting all the time, not only to manage your wealth, but also to continue to grow it, as you confidently move toward your financial goals.

However, the journey doesn't end here. Remember, wealth accumulation is a continuous process, a lifelong journey. Your ability to adapt, review, and adjust your financial plans is what will keep you on the path to financial prosperity.

Never forget the power of constant learning. Stay informed about the latest economic trends and financial strategies. Keep feeding your entrepreneurial spirit. Above all, keep growing your financial wisdom.

CHAPTER 5

The Wealth Hoarder

The New You

We've focused on how to grasp opportunities, harness wisdom, and navigate the intricate world of finance. We've talked about how every action, every conscious decision taken today, contributes to a better tomorrow.

Congratulations, by this point, you have now successfully evolved into a proficient Wealth Accumulator. Your financial acumen has grown exponentially, and you've mastered the art of making well-informed, rewarding decisions. Money, once a source of stress and uncertainty, has transformed into a tool for building a secure future.

The metamorphosis you've experienced hasn't been limited to your financial outlook alone. It has positively permeated into all spheres of your life. You may have noticed a more fulfilling relationship with your spouse, children, or parents, marked by a sense of security and mutual growth. With newfound wisdom, you now discern between needs and wants more effectively, enhancing your personal satisfaction and life contentment.

Your social circle too has evolved, now filled with individuals who contribute positively to your life, adding value with each interaction. You've embraced the joys of simple living and high thinking, feeling happier than ever before.

Another aspect of this transformation is your heightened sense of time management. You now have a surplus of time, which you've learned to organize more productively. You've indulged in new activities, embraced fresh routines, and generally feel more energetic and vivacious.

With this financial independence, you now have the luxury of choice—choosing the work you love, choosing to retire early, choosing to assist others. And this choice extends beyond the present. You're building a legacy that can impact generations, a topic we'll explore further as we delve into wills, trusts, and financial education for children.

This chapter, dear reader, is all about embracing this 'new you'. It's about acknowledging the growth, celebrating transformation, and setting forth towards the future with renewed enthusiasm and wisdom.

Remember, this journey of wealth accumulation is not just about you, but about every life you touch and inspire. This is your story, your transformation. Welcome to the new 'you.'

The Impact of Wealth Accumulation on Your Life

Accumulating wealth isn't merely about the increase in the number of zeros in our bank account, but about the multitude of personal benefits and substantial changes it brings about in our lives.

Remember the sleepless nights fretting over mounting bills, or the knots in your stomach each time an unexpected expense arose? Well, my dear reader, successful wealth accumulation diminishes these stressors. It brings about financial security and independence that you'd perhaps only dreamed of in the past. It gives you the freedom to make choices, the liberty to spend on things that matter without compromising your financial stability.

Let's take a moment to delve into the sense of security that wealth accumulation brings. Imagine not worrying about living paycheck to paycheck or stressing about funding your child's college education. Envision the liberation of knowing that your golden years are secure, that retirement isn't a ticking time bomb but a well-deserved restful period of your life. That's the magic of wealth accumulation.

Financial stress can exact a heavy toll on health. Your mastery over your finances can thus lead to improvements in your physical and mental wellbeing, making you feel more energetic and less anxious.

But the impact doesn't end there. There's a certain peace of mind and a myriad of opportunities that come along with it. The peace of mind stems from the comfort of knowing that your financial future is secure, that you are prepared for the unexpected, and that you have a safety net to fall back on. You now sleep better, wake up refreshed, and find that you can enjoy the simple pleasures of life without the cloud of financial worries hovering above.

Finally, with the stability you've achieved, you can afford experiences previously out of reach. Whether it is traveling to new places, getting to know new cultures or trying different hobbies, these experiences will broaden your perspective and enrich your life in unexpected ways.

Then come the opportunities. Ah, the exciting part of the journey! As your wealth grows, doors begin to open. You could invest in a new business venture, explore an early retirement, or fulfill a long-cherished dream of a world tour. The horizon of possibilities stretches far and wide, and you get to choose the path.

The most beautiful part of this journey, however, is that you're not only changing your life but also creating a legacy. You're setting an example for your children, your friends, even for those who doubted you. And in the process, you're inspiring them to embark on their own journeys towards financial independence.

The extent of the impact that your accumulation of wealth can have is, in fact, beyond your imagination. To illustrate, let's consider an example. As your wealth expands, your purchasing habits evolve. Perhaps you now have the resources to refurbish your home to your exact preferences. In embarking on this endeavor, you inadvertently set off a ripple effect of prosperity.

By investing money in this renovation project, you are benefiting the contractor hired for the job and their employees. This not only boosts their livelihoods but also fuels their ability to spend and invest in their own lives. The supplier of the materials reaps the benefits too, seeing increased sales and having the opportunity to reinvest profits back into their business, perhaps hiring more staff or expanding their product range.

Then there's the delivery person, whose income is fortified with your purchase. Even the fuel station where they fill their delivery vehicle's tank feels the impact. The ripples continue, flowing outward from you, touching lives in ways you might not even realize.

In essence, your personal journey to wealth accumulation does more than just securing your financial future; it stimulates your local economy, supports jobs, and contributes to community growth. Your decision years ago to embark on the path to hoarding wealth is now facilitating a cycle of prosperity that benefits many. It's a testament to the expansive power of wealth, not just to transform your own life, but to uplift those around you, directly and indirectly.

Inspiring Others on Their Wealth Accumulation Journey

Just as a stone thrown into a pond creates ripples, your successful journey of wealth accumulation has the power to influence and inspire those around you. The positive changes in your life, the financial freedom you've attained, the peace of mind you've achieved - all of these are not just personal victories, but also valuable lessons for those who aspire to embark on a similar journey.

You've seen the transformation firsthand, haven't you? The late nights of planning, the sacrifices you made, the discipline you cultivated - and the results they brought. These experiences carry a powerful message and sharing them can be the spark that ignites the path for others.

Now, think about your family, your friends, your colleagues. Picture their faces and ask yourself, 'Wouldn't it be wonderful if they could also experience this financial freedom?' That's where you come in. You can show them that it's possible, that they, too, can change their financial narratives.

Your journey has the potential to inspire your children and teach them about financial responsibility from an early age. You can foster in them the habit of saving, the knowledge of investing, and the wisdom of planning for their financial future.

Your success story can also influence your peers, showing them that it is never too late to start the journey towards financial independence. Whether it's a coworker, friend, or relative, your example can encourage them to take that crucial first step.

Your financial transformation can affect the lives of those in your community and beyond. You can inspire more than your inner circle, you can inspire your colleagues, your workers, in the case of those who are business owners, and many others by sharing your experiences in small social conversations or as large as in workshops, seminars or even through social media. Your story can provide hope, guidance, and practical steps to help others change their financial destiny. It has the potential to echo far and wide, reaching people in places you might not have even imagined. You have the chance to share your knowledge, to provide guidance and to inspire others towards financial independence.

But let's not forget about the digital world. Today's technology allows us to connect with people all over the globe, and social media platforms can be a powerful tool to share your experiences and wisdom. Imagine the impact your story could have on someone who's thousands of miles away! It can provide them hope, inspire them to start their own journey, and offer practical steps to help them reshape their financial destiny.

You now have the capacity to help out friends or family in financial need without jeopardizing your own financial security. You can give generously to causes that resonate with you, contributing to the betterment of society. The joy and satisfaction that come from being able to use your wealth to make a positive difference in others' lives can be deeply fulfilling.

In essence, as a successful wealth accumulator, you are now in a unique position to not only enjoy the fruits of your labor but also to give back, to educate, and to inspire. It's a ripple effect that begins with you and has the potential to spread far and wide. You are now a beacon of hope and an embodiment of financial independence.

Securing Generational Wealth

"One day, you'll plant a tree under whose shade you do not plan to sit," goes a famous quote. This is the essence of generational wealth and the spirit of the legacy we hope to leave behind. Having walked the path of wealth accumulation, made prudent decisions, and built a robust financial standing, it's time to reflect on the seeds you're sowing for future generations.

Think of your wealth not as a static entity, but as a flourishing garden, where each investment is a seed you plant. Your planning, nurturing, and patience allow these seeds to grow, to bloom, and ultimately to bear fruit. This garden is not just for you to enjoy, but also for your children, their children, and the generations to come.

Generational wealth isn't about providing an endless supply of money; it's about creating opportunities. It's about opening doors for higher education, supporting entrepreneurial endeavors, helping purchase their first home, and much more. It allows the future generations to stand on your shoulders, to start where you finished rather than where you began, thus ascending to new heights.

The impact of generational wealth goes beyond financial security. It is a beacon of stability in an unpredictable world. It gives your descendants the freedom to follow their passions and dreams, free from financial constraints that might otherwise limit their choices. It is an enduring testament of your love, care, and foresight—a silent promise of support that extends beyond your lifetime.

But remember, along with wealth, it's critical to pass on the knowledge, values, and financial wisdom that led to its accumulation. Teaching future generations the principles of managing wealth responsibly, investing wisely, and giving generously is as important as the wealth itself.

Proper planning is key in this endeavor. This includes estate planning, creating a will, setting up trusts, and laying down clear guidelines for wealth management. It may also involve educating your family about financial matters, encouraging them to learn, engage, and participate in maintaining and growing the family wealth.

By preparing a well-structured plan for your wealth, you not only safeguard your family's future but also leave a legacy of financial empowerment. You enable the continued growth of the wealth you've accumulated, influencing lives and making a difference in ways you might never get to see. This is the gift of generational wealth—the gift of a brighter, secure, and more prosperous future for those who come after you.

Leaving a legacy of wealth is the last stage in your journey as a wealth accumulator, but it is perhaps the most meaningful one. For it is in giving that we receive, and through planning for future generations that we truly immortalize our financial success. After all, the tree you plant today could provide shade for many generations to come.

Continue Your Journey with Us

For more insights and knowledge, please visit our website:

https://hoardingwealth.com

Become a valued member of our community. Engage, share, and learn with peers:

Join Our Community: **https://hoardingwealth.com/register/**

Access specialized financial tools and calculators to enhance your financial understanding:

Resource Center: **https://hoardingwealth.com/resources/**

Your journey to financial mastery begins here.

Index